WHO NEEDS IT

church?

SKIP HEITIZIG

WHO church? NEEDS IT

SKIP HEITIZIG

Alachua, Florida 32615

Bridge-Logos
Alachua, FL 32615 USA

Church: Who Needs It?
by Skip Heitzig

Printed in the United States of America.

Library of Congress Catalog Card Number Pending
International Standard Book Number 978-0-88270-730-3

Dedication

Dedicated to the church body
at Calvary of Albuquerque...

Your hunger for truth and dedication to Jesus Christ

has been a testimony to our community.

Your faith and works have been felt

throughout the world.

CONTENTS

CHAPTER 1

How to Go to Church

AND THRIVE

Americans tend to shop for churches just like they shop for clothes and cars. When you look across the church landscape, there is a multitude of confusing choices. Whether that's a good or bad thing, I'll leave for you to decide. But without question, there are a lot of options from which to choose in the church landscape of America.

We have loud churches and quiet ones, old ones and young ones, fun ones and more than a few boring ones. Some services last what many would consider an inordinate amount of time, while others fly by, often featuring sermonettes rather than expositional teaching.

The wide variety of church options brings up a fundamental question: "What do I want in a church? What am I looking for in an assembly of believers?" What *you* look for probably depends a great deal on where you came from. Since we have different backgrounds, we value diverse traditions.

I grew up Roman Catholic; I met the Lord when I was eighteen-years-old. My wife grew up agnostic. Others have grown up atheistic. Still others came of age in a wide assortment of churches and denominations. This means we come to church with different kinds of baggage and varying ideas of what church "ought to be."

While it's important to ask, "What do I think church should be?" it's far more important to ask another question. I think too often we fail to ask the Church's founder and director, Jesus Christ—the One whose idea "church" was to begin with—what *He* thinks it should be. It's His Church, after all. So what does *Jesus* think the church should be?

Back to the Source

From a New Testament perspective, what is "church" all about? Why do we gather on Sundays, schedule meetings for other times, put together programs, sing songs, hold outreaches, and all the rest? Why do church at all?

And once we choose to do it, how can we survive it, then thrive in it?

I know quite a few people who go to church and don't survive. They don't make it for a number of reasons that we'll consider as we move through this book. But right out of the chute, I want us to look closely at Jesus' take on the church. He first spoke of it immediately after asking His disciples a probing question that stumped most of them. Matthew writes:

> *When Jesus came into the region of Caesarea Philippi, He asked His disciples, saying, "Who do men say that I, the Son of Man, am?" So they said, "Some say John the Baptist, some Elijah, and others Jeremiah or one of the prophets." He said to them, "But who do you say that I am?" Simon Peter answered and said, "You are the Christ, the Son of the living God." Jesus answered and said to him, "Blessed are you, Simon Bar-Jonah, for flesh and blood has not revealed this*

> *to you, but My Father who is in heaven. And I also say to you that you are Peter, and on this rock I will build My church, and the gates of Hades shall not prevail against it."* (Matthew 16:13-18)

This passage highlights four fundamental truths that will help us not only to survive church but also to thrive in it.

The Church: Its Designation

Jesus calls His new creation the "Church." He declares, "Upon this rock I will build My *church.*" That's the designation He gives it.

The New Testament uses the term "church" more than one hundred times in either its plural or singular forms. It makes its first appearance in Matthew 16:18, and the first mention of anything in Scripture is worth studying carefully in its context to find out exactly what it means.

To the modern ear, the word "church" has some definite (and not always positive) connotations. We tend to think of it as a religious word or creation. Some would call it an outdated religious idea. Mention the word "church," and many people immediately think of a structure of stone, wood, or stucco with steeples, crosses, and bells. Others see in their mind's eye a solemn institution filled with frowning old men wearing black robes with stiff, white collars.

Yet the term "church" has entirely secular roots. The ancient Greeks created it as a governmental word referring to an assembly of citizens. They used the term *ecclesia* to refer to an assembly of Greek citizens who met regularly at some public place. As time went on, it meant a legislative body that met regularly.

Acts 19 tells of a near riot in Ephesus after the Apostle Paul preached the gospel there. Thousands of angry Ephesians crowded into the city's huge 25,000-seat theater and for two hours cried out, *"Great is Diana of the Ephesians! Great is Diana of the Ephesians!"* (v. 28). The city clerk finally quieted the unruly mob and said, *"If you have any other inquiry to make, it shall be determined in the lawful assembly"* (v. 39). Luke adds, *"And when he had said these things, he dismissed the assembly"* (v. 41). Both times, the word translated "assembly" is the Greek term *ecclesia*.

The word we know as "church" originally came from the union of two Greek terms. It's a combination of the word *ek*, which means "out of" or "from," and the word *kaleo*, which means "to call." When you put the two terms together, you create a word that means "to call out from." So the original idea of the church (the *ecclesia*) was a people called out from their society to meet for their own common good and purpose.

That's what a church is: *a group of people called out from the rest of the community to meet for a common goal and purpose.* Jesus' choice of this term is very revealing.

First, it reveals that Jesus does not want His followers to remain isolated individuals. Quite the opposite! He wants them to form an integrated community designed for encouragement and support. Jesus didn't say, "You are Peter, and upon this rock I will build My monastery." Nor did He say, "You are Peter, and upon this rock I will build My private place of meditation where you can pursue your own personal journey." Instead He said, "Upon this rock I'm going to build a unique assembly of people, called out from society to meet together so they might accomplish My purpose."

We've all heard people say, "I don't need church." It's almost the modern mantra: "I'm not into organized religion." Yet Jesus answers, "Wrong! You *do* need the church. Every Christian needs church—and every Christian is a part of My called-out Church."

Hebrews 10:24-25 says, "*And let us consider one another in order to stir up love and good works, not forsaking the assembling of ourselves together, as is the manner of some, but exhorting one another, and so much the more as you see the Day approaching.*"

Why is church so important? Solomon answers, "*A man who isolates himself seeks his own desire; he rages against all wise judgment*" (Proverbs 18:1). When you regularly fellowship with other Christians, you make it harder for yourself to live selfishly.

According to Jesus, the idea of "church" means that we're to follow Him as a community, as a unified group. He doesn't call us into an exclusively private and personal relationship with Him. He wants us to do things with one another—so it is no surprise that the term translated "one another" appears some seventy times in the New Testament. Jesus repeatedly calls us to develop close, encouraging relationships with fellow Christians in the church.

Of course, I can hear the question coming: "But can't I be a Christian without joining a church?" The technical answer is yes because the Bible makes it clear that when you put your faith in Christ and believe in your heart that God raised Him from the dead and confess with your mouth that Jesus is Lord, "you will be saved," to quote the Apostle Paul (see Romans 10:9). When you do that, you'll go to Heaven one day. So yes, you can be a Christian without joining a church.

But do you know what that's like? It's like . . .

being a soldier without an army;

being a sailor without a boat;

being a football player without a team;

being a tuba player without an orchestra;

being a bee without a hive.

Yes, you can get by without the church—but you won't get by very well. And for no good reason you'll make yourself unnecessary prey to temptation and to destructive forces in the world that want to do you harm. Can you be a Christian without getting involved in a local church? Sure. You'll just be an unhappy, ineffective, disobedient, at risk, and very foolish one.

Second, Jesus wants His followers to stand out from the dominant culture. If the term *ecclesia* refers to a group of called-out people who assemble to accomplish a common goal, then it seems obvious that they are to be different from those who are not "called out." Believers in Christ who gather for worship are not simply a group of religious men and women who meet to sing and pray and quote Bible verses. Jesus calls us to be a *holy* assembly, both when we're assembled and when we're apart.

Additionally, we are not to copy the world or to try to prove to others in society, "Hey, we're as cool as you are! We're as hip as you are! See, we can do what you do. We're just called a Christian group." Jesus says we're to be distinctly *different* from the world. And what makes us different? We love Jesus supremely. *That's* what makes us different.

So is there some rule about how often we should assemble as a church? People frequently ask me, "Skip, how often do I have to go to church?"

"Wrong question," I usually answer. It's not a matter of how often you *have* to go, but rather, how often you *want* to go. I think that's a good indication of who you really are inside.

One Sunday morning a couple saw it was time to get ready for church. The wife got up, dressed, and was almost out the door when she noticed her husband continuing to turn over in bed.

"Honey, get up!" she said. "It's time to go to church."

"I'm not going to church today," he replied.

"You're not going to church?" she wondered aloud. "How come?"

"I have three reasons," he answered. "Number one, the people in that church are cold and unloving; number two, nobody likes me there; and number three, I don't feel like going."

"Well," she replied, "let me give you three good reasons why you should go to church. Number one, the people in this church are warm, friendly, and loving; number two, I can think of a few people who like you; and number three, you're the pastor! So get up and let's go to church!"

I can assure you, I've been there!

I grew up going to church out of cold, hard duty. They used to tell us, "It's your Sunday obligation." So I looked at God as an obligation. Contrast that with my wife, Lenya. After she came to know Christ, you couldn't *keep* her away from church! She went literally every night they held a service.

Why do some believers look at "assembling together" as an unpleasant duty or as something to grudgingly attempt every once in a while? Why do so many seem to say, "Okay, since it's Christmas, I'll go," or, "It's a wedding for a friend, so I guess I'll make it to church"? Why does it seem you have to drag some people to church, while others have to be dragged out, because they love it so much?

We can all probably name any number of reasons, but one in particular stands out to me. I'll even quote it from Scripture:

> *We know that we have passed from death to life, because we love the brethren. He who does not love his brother abides in death* (1 John 3:14).

When you show that you love other Christians by joyfully assembling together with them, you prove that you have passed from death to life. But if you stay away from them, how can you love them? And if you don't love them, then you're still spiritually dead, biblically speaking.

Let me say it this way: The way you treat God's kids reveals a lot about the way you treat God. And God says, "If you say you love Me, then you had better love My children."

At the bottom line, that's what "church" is all about.

The Church: Its Foundation

What were the foundational principles Jesus used when He started the Church? Did He establish it on the strength and character of His disciples? Or did He build it on the foundation of good marketing, slick advertising, and snazzy packaging? Look again at verses 16-18 of Matthew 16.

> *Simon Peter answered and said, "You are the Christ, the Son of the living God." Jesus answered and said to him, "Blessed are you, Simon Bar-Jonah, for flesh and blood has not revealed this to you, but My Father who is in heaven. And I also say to you that you are Peter, and on this rock I will build My church, and the gates of Hades shall not prevail against it."*

I think too many of us take a lot of cheap potshots at Peter. I suspect a long line of preachers will assemble in Heaven to say to the apostle, "I'm sorry, Peter, for all the nasty things I've said about you." Yes, he did fail; yes, he was weak. But here he stands tall! He's the only guy in the group who got an A on the test.

"Who do you say that I am?" Jesus asked His disciples.

Only Peter gave the right answer: "You are the Christ, the Son of the living God."

Bingo! Right on Simon, son of Jonah. You heard directly from God on that one! "Flesh and blood didn't reveal this to you," Jesus assured him, "but My Father who is in heaven." So far, so good—but then a lot of us get tripped up by what Jesus said next.

"On this rock," Jesus declared, "I will build My church." More than a few people have puzzled over that statement. What exactly did Jesus mean? On what "rock" would He build His Church?

The tradition I grew up in identifies Peter as the rock. It considers him and his leadership as the foundation stone of the Church. Upon Peter and his apostleship, this view claims, Jesus built His Church.

But what a weak Church that would be! And if Peter were here, I think he'd say, "Amen to that." To build any divine organization on a mere man—even one as remarkable as Peter—is a weak strategy at best. And it's not as though Jesus had said, "Peter, you are such an incredible individual that I've decided to bet the entire future of My organization on you." No, that's not the idea here at all.

While the word Peter (*petros* in Greek) does mean "rock," it's not the kind of rock you may have in mind. Don't think of a huge, massive boulder. Think of a small nugget or a pebble. Don't think of Rocky Balboa saying, "Yo, thanks, Lord." Think instead of Pebbles from *The Flintstones*. *That's* Peter.

Let me paint the real picture for you.

Twenty-five miles north of the Sea of Galilee on a lush plain, Jesus spent most of His time with His disciples. An important city named Caesarea Philippi rose on that plain at the foot of the tallest mountain in the Middle East, Mount Hermon, which is more than 9,000 feet high. Caesarea Philippi also lay at the headwaters of the Jordan River. Even today part of the Jordan bursts forth from a massive rock near the ruins of Caesarea Philippi to water the entire land of Israel. Back then many Jews called it "the living water."

Caesarea Philippi was a place of stark contrasts. Not only did Jews revere it because of the Jordan, but others revered it as well. No fewer than fourteen pagan temples adorned the city. At one time, Baal worship flourished there. Greek mythology held that the god Paneas (Pan) was born there. Herod the Great built a temple to Caesar Augustus there. So Caesarea Philippi had become sacred to the Jews, to the Greeks, to the Romans, and to other pagans.

And *this* is where Jesus took His men. *This* is the backdrop of the story from Matthew. And this is where Jesus asked His men, "Who do you say that I am?" and where Peter replied, "You are the Christ, the Son of the living God."

When Jesus said, "You are Peter, and on this rock I will build My church," He was making a play on words that everyone at the time surely understood. They all knew about the massive rock from which the Jordan River gushed out; in Greek, that rock would have been called a *petra*. The name Peter (*petros*), on the other hand, means "a nugget" or "a small stone." So Jesus was saying, "You are *Petros* (a small stone), and upon this *petra* (a massive boulder) I will build My church."

So the question is, "What is the massive boulder upon which Jesus promised to build His Church?" If Peter isn't it, what is? Well, look around the text; what massive rock do you see nearby? Peter had just spoken it: "You are the Christ, the Son of the living God." It's hard to get much bigger than *that!* So, in essence, Jesus replied, "Peter, you're right! I don't want you to ever forget this moment or this truth. So I'm going to make it easy for you to remember by giving you a name that will remind you that you're a little chip off the old Block. Peter, you're a pebble (*petros*), and upon this rock (*petra*) of truth—upon this massive confession that you just made, that I am the Christ, the Son of the Living God—I am going to build My Church."

The Church isn't built on puny Peter the pebble, but on massive Mount Messiah. It's built on the Solid Rock, Jesus Christ. So the Apostle Paul wrote, *"For no other foundation can anyone lay than that which is laid, which is Jesus Christ"* (1 Corinthians 3:11).

Do you really want to survive church? If so, then get your eyes off of people—whether it's Peter or a pastor or a board—and fix your eyes on Jesus Christ.

Jesus has something far more fundamental in mind here than mere survival, however. The issue isn't merely surviving church, but thriving in church. So let me ask a question: Are you just coming to church?

"What do you mean," someone says, "*just* coming to church? It takes a lot of effort to come to church!" Yes, it does—especially if you're coming merely to church, rather than to meet with Jesus Christ.

Are you resting on the solid rock foundation that is Jesus Christ? You can be baptized in a church, married in a church, and even sing or preach in a church, but if from your heart you can't confess that Jesus is your Lord, then you are *not* a part of it. In that case, you just go to church; you merely attend it. You might be resting on membership in some church, but you're not building upon the rock of Jesus Christ and enjoying a living, dynamic relationship with Him.

Paul once spoke of a group of people *"having a form of godliness but denying its power"* (2 Timothy 3:5). The New Living Translation renders this verse, *"They will act as if they are religious, but they will reject the power that could make them godly."* Paul also warned Titus about people who *"profess to know God, but in works they deny Him"* (Titus 1:16). It's possible to be in church, but not of it.

So, how do you take full advantage of this living body that Jesus created for your own good? How do you get active in church, survive church, and thrive in church? You begin by recognizing what it is (a body of believers called out to live for Christ) and what it is built on (the Rock of God, Mount Messiah).

God has called out every one of us from the world, to stand out in both holiness and love. We are to be different from those who don't know Christ—not judgmental or harsh or loony. Instead we should be so distinct in our outlook and behavior that people will know we "have been with Jesus" (see Acts 4:13). Jesus calls us to be integrated with each other in joy and in peace. What ties us together is our common confession that Jesus Christ is our Lord, our Rock of salvation.

The Church: Its Possession

We often say, "Come to my church" or "Let's visit Dr. X's church." Or maybe you say to others, "Hey, why don't you come with me to our church?" While there's nothing wrong with that, we have to remember whose church it really is.

It's His!

The Church is the possession of Jesus Christ, not of anyone else. That means Jesus doesn't have to clear His decisions with Rome, with London, with Minneapolis, with Costa

Mesa, or with any other place or authority. *He* is the authority. It is *His* Church. *He* is the founder. *He* is the director. *He* is the One who thought it all up. The Church is *His* possession.

Do you like mysteries? A lot of people do—and the Bible has more than a few of them. One of the greatest mysteries concerns the Church. Nowhere in the Old Testament was the Church revealed, according to the Apostle Paul. It was kept a secret, a mystery, until after the time of Jesus. The Church was God's plan from the beginning, but God kept it hidden until He chose to reveal it. Today, the Church is no longer a mystery. The secret has been revealed, and it belongs to Jesus, because He thought of it.

Not only did Jesus think up the Church, but He also bought the Church with His own blood. When Paul approached the elders of the church in Ephesus, the apostle exhorted them, "*. . . shepherd the church of God which He purchased with His own blood*" (Acts 20:28). And when Paul wrote to the church in Corinth, he said, "*Do you not know that your body is the temple of the Holy Spirit who is in you, whom you have from God, and you are not your own? For you were bought at a price; therefore glorify God in your body and in your spirit, which are God's*" (1 Corinthians 6:19-20).

So if Jesus bought the Church with His own blood and redeemed us with His own life, then it's His Church. Every pastor of every church and every member of every church board should remember that *the church belongs to Jesus.* That reminder would take a load off of us all!

In the same way, every Christian in every church should remember that Christ owns the church. What a difference that would make! When we gather at various times, we also need to remember that God owns every person sitting next to us (so long as they're believers). Those are blood-bought believers around us! So we ought to think twice about criticizing each other or passing judgment on other churches down the block or across town. Remember—Jesus bought them, too.

First Thessalonians opens with these words: *"Paul, Silvanus, and Timothy, to the church of the Thessalonians in God the Father and the Lord Jesus Christ."* We belong to Jesus, whether we sit in pews in a church building or sprawl on the floor of a house church. If we have a relationship with God through faith in Jesus Christ, we belong to Him. He bought us. That is why we must be *very* careful about how we talk about God's Church. Consider what it cost Jesus to purchase it!

The Church: Its Preservation

Sometimes, when we hear about a well-known pastor who has flamed out sexually or we read of a poll that suggests organized religion is in trouble, we wonder about the health and survival of the church. We worry, "Are we in trouble? Is the church in danger of dying out? Does God's work need rescuing?"

The answer, according to Jesus, is *no*. Remember His words: *"I will build My church, and the gates of Hades shall not prevail against it"* (Matthew 16:18).

Throughout history, various men and women have stood up to mock the church. In 1776, the skeptic David Hume said, "I can see the twilight of Christianity." The poor guy couldn't tell the difference between a sunset and a sunrise! The church was just getting started in this country.

The French infidel Voltaire made a brash prediction that Christianity would become extinct within one hundred years of his writings. Well…not exactly. Within fifty years of his death, the Geneva Bible Society was using his former home to distribute Bibles throughout Europe. Isn't that *great*? God really does have a sense of humor.

The gates of hell will not prevail against the Church of Jesus Christ!

Nevertheless, I'd be lying if I said we had no room for concern. Every year in Europe, for example, about eighty-two churches close, and their former properties are being converted into public buildings or even into mosques, as in Bradford, England. They sell the old pews as antique furniture; it's become very popular. A lot of people think it's cool to put a former church baptistery in the front yard and use it as a birdbath.

Thank God that in other parts of the world, fires of revival continue to burn! South America has seen an explosion of church growth in the past couple of decades, while in less than fifty years the Church in China has grown from one million members to over eighty million.[1]

[1]And do you know the common denominator to all this church growth? It's not marketing. It's persecution. Most of the time, when officials persecute a group of believers, that church will grow. I'm going to say something very bold, something you may not want to hear. *If you really want to pray for growth, then pray for a little persecution.* Why? Because persecution will quickly separate the chaff from the wheat. The strong will emerge, and Jesus will use them to build His Church.

When Jesus hung on the cross some 2,000 years ago, many observers no doubt looked on and said, "Well, it's over. Christianity is finished. Its founder is dying, so I guess that's that." They would have been very wrong. That dark

1. See Endnotes, page 247.

event marked the beginning because in just a few days *HE WAS BACK!*

And He's been moving in power ever since.

When Jesus declared, "I will build My church," He meant that you could open up the doors of hell and unleash every vile demon to attack the Church—be it persecution, death, or burning down buildings—and it simply will not go away.

"I'm going to do My work," Jesus says, "and nothing and nobody will stop Me."

Are We As He Wants Us?

Do you remember the Jesus Movement? I do. I recall fondly how Jesus moved in remarkable ways—and so I've begun praying for a new movement, a rekindling, a revival.

Jesus is still moving—and I want to be a part of it. I want to see another movement of God!

May I ask you a question? If everyone in church were just like you, then what kind of church would it be? Would it be a revival just waiting to happen or a bunch of sleepy waiters desperately in need of revival?

The late Dr. James Kennedy once wrote, "Most people think of the church as a drama in which the minister is the chief actor, God is the prompter, and the laity is the critic. What is actually the case is that the congregation is the chief actor, the minister is the prompter, and God is the critic."[2]

So let's ask the Lord: "Are we what You want us to be?"

2. See Endnotes, page 247.

CHAPTER 2

A Church of Glory

AND TRUTH

I recently came across some interesting job descriptions for church staff positions. I'm not quite sure if they should make me laugh or cry:

- *Pastor:* able to leap tall buildings in a single bound; more powerful than a locomotive; faster than a speeding bullet; walks on water; and gives counsel to God.
- *Assistant Pastor:* able to leap short buildings in a single bound; as powerful as a switch engine; just as fast as a speeding bullet; walks on water when the sea is calm; and talks with God.
- *Music Minister:* leaps short buildings with a running start; almost as powerful as a switch engine; faster than a speeding BB; is occasionally addressed by God; and walks on water if he or she knows where the tree stumps are.
- *Youth Minister*: runs into small buildings; recognizes locomotives two out of three times; uses a squirt gun; knows how to use the water fountain; and mumbles to himself.

- *Church Secretary*: lifts buildings to walk under them; kicks locomotives off the track; catches speeding bullets in her teeth; freezes water with a single glance; and when God speaks she says, "May I ask who's calling?"[1]

The person who wrote these descriptions obviously knows something about the internal workings of most American churches. I find the descriptions funny because I can see a definite element of truth in each one. Yet how many people read them and don't laugh at all, mainly because these folks totally misperceive both the church at large and her flawed staff people?

During a recent visit to Washington, DC, I began a conversation with a woman named Natalie. She had recently moved to the United States from Belarus and had settled in Chicago. She talked about her difficult transition from her own culture to this one. When I asked about her relationship with the Lord, she replied, "I go to a church—but even church seems cold, uncaring, and irrelevant." She paused for a moment and then declared, "I believe in God… but I don't believe in church."

In other words, "Jesus, yes. Church, no."

Immediately after that conversation, I hailed a cab headed for Georgetown. In the taxi I asked the driver, who was from Ethiopia, about his relationship with the Lord. He told me that he was a Christian, that he belonged to the Ethiopian Orthodox Church, and that he also had left his country and his biological family. But the similarities to Natalie ended there. "I love going to church," he enthused. "It's my *family*!"

---

1. See Endnotes, page 247

In just a few minutes, I had spoken with two people from different parts of the world with opposite experiences in church. One hated it; one loved it. Why the big difference? And what *should* church be, according to Jesus?

A Remarkable Prayer

What does Jesus want His Church to be? We get some solid indications in John 17, the longest recorded prayer of Jesus in the New Testament.

Jesus prayed on many occasions, of course. He often got up early in the morning to pray or would spend all night in prayer to God. But in John 17, as He looks to the future and recognizes He's about to leave His disciples, He prays a very special prayer—one His disciples got to hear Him pray out loud.

As we work through this prayer and hear what Jesus requests from His Father, we begin to understand what Jesus wants for His Church. In this chapter we'll investigate two basic qualities that Jesus wants to see in His Church.

Radiate the Glory of God

The first thing Jesus wants to see in His Church might surprise you. It's not specifically about any of the things you might expect—evangelism, upright behavior, missions, teaching. Let's begin in verse 1 and see how Jesus wants the church *to radiate the glory of God*:

> *Jesus spoke these words, lifted up His eyes to heaven, and said: "Father, the hour has come. Glorify Your Son, that Your Son also may glorify You, as You have given Him authority over all flesh, that He should give eternal life to as many as You have given Him.*

> *And this is eternal life, that they may know You, the only true God, and Jesus Christ whom You have sent. I have glorified You on the earth. I have finished the work which You have given Me to do. And now, O Father, glorify Me together with Yourself, with the glory that I had with You before the world was. I have manifested Your name to the men whom You have given Me out of the world. They were Yours, You gave them to Me, and they have kept Your word."* (vv. 1-6)
>
> *"I pray for them. I do not pray for the world but for those whom You have given Me, for they are Yours. And all Mine are Yours, and Yours are Mine, and I am glorified in them."* (vv. 9-10)
>
> *"And the glory which You gave Me I have given them, that they may be one just as We are one."* (v. 22)
>
> *"Father, I desire that they also whom You gave Me may be with Me where I am, that they may behold My glory which You have given Me; for You loved Me before the foundation of the world."* (v. 24)

Eight times in this passage the word "glory," or "glorify," appears. But what does it mean? You rarely hear the word outside of church; it has a definite religious, stained-glass sound to it. By using it, what is Jesus trying to communicate to us?

The Meaning of "Glory"

It's vital that we understand the meaning of the term "glory" because it's central to the prayer. It's equally central to what drove Jesus Christ in His life and to what Jesus wants us, His Church, to be. So what should we understand when we read the word "glory" (or "glorify")? The term means one of two things, and sometimes both:

1. *Glory describes the visible expression of God.*

"Glory" is the outward "WOW!" that surrounds the presence of God. It's what you'd expect to see whenever God shows up. Every time God appears in all His majesty and splendor, overpowering glory follows. It's stunning, bright, rapturous, blinding.

Think of the overwhelming experience Dorothy and her three pals had when they showed up in the emerald green halls of the great Wizard of Oz. It's like that, only a billion trillion gazillion times more intense.

Moses once prayed to see the glory of God. *"Please, show me Your glory,"* he asked the Lord (Exodus 33:18). God graciously replied, "Moses, My friend, no man can see My face and live. You'd be toast, buddy boy! But I will make all My goodness pass before you" (see Exodus 33:20-23). God kept His word and Moses got an amazing peek at a small portion of the Lord's glory. But even that glimpse was so intense that the Bible says, *"So Moses made haste and bowed his head toward the earth, and worshiped"* (Exodus 34:8).

You would, too.

The prophet Isaiah saw God's glory in a vision when he observed the Lord high and lifted up, with the train of His robe filling the Temple. The angels in his vision proclaimed, *"Holy, holy, holy is the LORD of hosts; the whole earth is full of His glory!"* (Isaiah 6:3). Thus exposed to God's glory, *even in a vision*, Isaiah responded much as Moses had: *"Woe is me, for I am undone! Because I am a man of unclean lips, and I dwell in the midst of a people of unclean lips; for my eyes have seen the King, the LORD of hosts"* (v. 5). That's a picture of God's glory—the outward, visible expression of His majesty, holiness, and power.

2. *Glory describes valued attention toward God.*

The word "glory" conveyed a second idea that we give our focus and undivided attention to God in order to bring Him praise. When we do that, we can say, "I am glorifying God."

The word in Greek, *doxazo*, means "to have a good opinion of" or "to make renowned or valuable." So in verse 4 of His prayer, Jesus says, *"I have glorified You on the earth."* He means that through His words and His conduct, He has accurately painted a compelling picture of the true nature of God, resulting in praise to the Lord.

The idea is further developed in verse 6 when He says, *"I have manifested Your name."* Here He means something like this: "Father, by the way I have lived I put You at center stage. I've opened up the curtains and directed the spotlight to shine on You. It's all about You! And that's the value I've passed on to My disciples. I have made You number one in everything—I have glorified You by showcasing You in everything—and I have given them the same directive."

This is clearly what the Apostle Paul had in mind when he wrote, *"Whether you eat or drink, or whatever you do, do all to the glory of God"* (1 Corinthians 10:31).

The Primary Purpose of the Church

In our lives as individuals we are to bring glory to God. But is that also the purpose of the church? And if not, then what is its purpose? That question has been debated for centuries in the hallowed hallways of seminaries and churches. What is the primary purpose of the church? What's paramount?

Some would say, "World evangelism has to top the list, because Jesus told us to 'go and preach the gospel to the whole world.'" To this I would reply, "Certainly that is vital. Clearly it is important—but it's not number one."

Others would answer, "It's discipleship. It's teaching people to love and obey God—that's the primary mission of the church." To this I would reply, "Again, that's clearly important because Jesus told us to 'make disciples of all nations.' But still, it's not the main purpose of the church."

So what *is* the purpose of the church? The first and paramount role of the church, according to Jesus, is *to glorify God.* We are to bring glory to the Lord by shining the spotlight on Him, first and foremost.

In the Great Commission, Jesus told us to *"Go therefore and make disciples of all the nations, baptizing them in the name of the Father and of the Son and of the Holy Spirit, teaching them to observe all things that I have commanded you"* (Matthew 28:19-20). Yet before we can carry out the Great Commission, number one on our list must be obedience to the Great Commandment: *"You shall love the LORD your God with all your heart, with all your soul, with all your strength, and with all your mind"* (Luke 10:27). Great Devotion—devotion that motivates us to glorify God in all that we do—must precede everything else. It is the number one task of the church.

At Calvary Chapel of Albuquerque as we formed a purpose statement for our fellowship, we tried to keep this in mind:

- Upreach
- Inreach
- Outreach

Those three little words sum up our vision.

Upreach is why we are here, to bring glory and honor in our relationship with God. That's first and foremost.

Out of our growing relationship with the Lord come the strength and the ability to *inreach.* This is where we train, feed, equip, and bless one another in the body of Christ.

Only then can we begin to *outreach* or move into the world with the love of Jesus.

The primary goal of the Church must always remain the same: to point to God, to give focused attention to the Lord, to make Him known, and to enhance people's opinions of God as they witness our godly lifestyles. That's it! That's what it means to glorify God—and the Lord wants His Church to radiate His glory, first and foremost.

A Billboard or a Road Sign?

As you travel on most paved roads in this country, you encounter several kinds of markers. One is a billboard. A billboard is usually some type of flashy advertisement. The idea is to get you to focus on that billboard, because the advertiser wants to send you a message about some product or service.

A second kind of common marker is a road sign. Such a sign gives you helpful or vital information about what's coming up. It will say "Twenty Miles to . . . " or "Beware of Dangerous Curves" or "Reduced Speed Ahead." It's about travel conditions.

The first kind of marker draws attention to itself; the second kind points to something beyond itself.

The world would have you become a billboard: "Here I am! Look at me! Aren't I something?" It wants you to be all about *you*. God would rather have you and I serve as road signs pointing to Him: "He's working over here! He's like this!" We're all about *Him*.

A popular New York author's book proclaims *How to Be Your Own Best Friend*. I think that captures pretty well what the world considers to be the right personal goal in life: How to be your OWN best friend. *You* are the center of the universe! We see this warped idea in nearly all of our advertising. Consider the following classic slogans from popular companies:

- *McDonald's:* "You deserve a break today."
- *Nissan:* "Everything you want, nothing you don't."
- *Canon:* "Image is everything."
- *Pepsi*: "Drink Pepsi-Cola. It will satisfy you."
- *Sprite:* "Obey your thirst."
- *Toyota*: "You asked for it, you got it. Toyota."
- *Microsoft*: "Where do you want to go today?"

Why such an emphasis? Simply because advertisers know fallen human nature. They've studied it. They know that our natural human fabric seeks to glorify and satisfy ourselves rather than our Creator—and hence the unrelenting focus on pampering and catering to our own lusts and wants and desires.

Unfortunately, this warped emphasis has spilled over into some Christian circles. A false and destructive theology has sprung up that says, "Use faith to get whatever you want in life. Focus on something that you want and say, 'I claim it in Jesus' name. Hallelujah, it's mine.'" You identify it, you name it, and you claim it.

When you take this attitude, you reduce God to the level of a cosmic bellhop: "Our Concierge who art in Heaven." It's all about *me*. "This is what I want. This is what I demand. This is what You need to do for me, God." All I have to do is say, "Amen," at the end of my instructions, and it's mine.

I have a big problem with this focus. My Bible says everything that exists—Heaven and Earth and every last atom and electron in all creation—was created for God's pleasure (see Revelation 4:11). This verse clarifies that our primary purpose in life is to give glory and pleasure to God. It's *not* about me; it's about *Him.*

In the church, we have a huge challenge as we live in the midst of a "me" generation—our primary task is to become a "He" generation.

The Point of Worship

How do we move from a "me" focus to a "He" focus? While a number of things can help, one of the biggest is regular immersion in God-centered worship.

Worship is a fantastic way to get the attention off of "me" and onto "Him," the Lord of glory—that is, if it's true worship. Unfortunately, we have a way of making even worship about us.

"I didn't like that song—it was too loud."

"I didn't like that chorus—it was too soft."

"I like drums."

"I like the choir."

"I don't like the choir."

Who cares? Remember, it's about Him. *We're* not the audience! There's an audience of One, and that's the Lord.

Way back in 1928, Evelyn Underhill warned the Church of England, "We are drifting towards a religion which consciously or unconsciously keeps its eye on humanity rather than on Deity."[2] Let me announce something to you: We're no longer drifting; we've arrived.

We need to get back to the emphasis of even earlier church leaders. The Westminster Shorter Catechism (1647) asked

2. See Endnotes, page 247

the question, "What is the chief end of man?" It answered, "The chief end of man is to know God and to glorify Him forever."

So, what does Jesus want the church to be? Above all else… *We are to radiate the glory of God.*

Reveal the Truth of God

A second major purpose of the church is to reveal the truth of God. By giving attention to this second purpose of the church, we also give glory to God and thus help to fulfill our first purpose as the church.

Go back to Jesus' prayer in John 17. As He speaks to His Father about glorifying Him, note His emphasis on revealing God's truth:

> *I have manifested Your name to the men whom You have given Me out of the world. They were Yours, you gave them to Me and they have kept Your word. Now they have known that all things which You have given Me are from You. For I have given to them the words which You have given Me and they have received them and have known surely that I came forth from You; and they have believed that You sent Me.* (vv. 6-8)

If you've been around church for any time at all, no doubt you've heard some questions being asked by visitors and maybe even by some regular attenders: "Why is the service basically the same every week? You sing, you have a prayer, you sing a few more songs. Then that guy gets up and just keeps talking about the Bible. I mean, why don't you just have an interpretive dance one week or a raffle or something else fun? Why such a focus on the Bible?"

Here's the real question that needs to be asked: What did Jesus intend the church to be? Is it primarily a meeting place to make social connections? We get a big clue when we listen to Him praying: "I have given to them [the disciples] the words which You have given Me and they have received them."

This is one of the primary purposes of church: to give God's people God's words—found in His Word, the Bible—in a way that they can receive them. The Apostle Paul knew what he was doing when he instructed a young pastor named Timothy, "*Devote yourself to the public reading of Scripture, to preaching and to teaching*" (1 Timothy 4:13 NIV).

A Common Thread

Many churches in America are biblically illiterate. They don't have a good handle on the principles of God's Word for living on this planet the way God wants us to live. Too many of us still think an epistle is the wife of an apostle.

The Church, according to Jesus, should focus on Him, worship Him, and learn of Him through the words of God found in the Bible. That's what Jesus prayed for—and what the early church practiced whenever they came together as the Body of Christ. Throughout the Book of Acts, we see a strong emphasis on the Word of God. When the apostles preached and taught, they always preached and taught from the Word.

And even beyond the Book of Acts, if you were to look back into Church history and examine all of the great movements of God—those times when faith made a resurgence in a decaying culture—you would see that all of them had a common element. Whether you studied the Moravian movement, the Wesleyan movement, the reforms of Martin Luther, the Great Awakening, the Second Great Awakening, the Welsh revival, or any other significant revival, you would find that they *all* brought out and amplified the teaching of the Word of God. That makes sense, because that was the very principle upon which the Church was built.

Acts 2:42 says, *"And they continued steadfastly in the apostles' doctrine and fellowship, in the breaking of bread, and in prayers."* What was number one on that list? The apostles' doctrine. Why? Why should *that* be number one? Why not loving or singing or praying? Why the apostles' doctrine? It's very simple: It is the Word of God that teaches you how to pray, how to love, how to raise your kids, how to sing the way God wants you to sing, etc. It *all* comes from the Word.

When the Church gives God's Word its proper place, God is pleased to bless it. Remember what He said through Isaiah the prophet? *"My word . . ."* He declared, *"shall not return to Me void, but it shall accomplish what I please, and it shall prosper in the thing for which I sent it"* (Isaiah 55:11). So it is no big surprise to read of the early church—the one that regularly preached and taught God's Word—*"And the Lord added to the church daily those who were being saved"* (Acts 2:47).

In fact, any church that doesn't put the Word of God first will become imbalanced, weak, ineffective, and confused. Guaranteed.

You Can't Do Without It

Once there was a small village with a clock in the center of town. The locals called it the *glockenspiel* and everyone in town set their watches by it.

One day, the glass enclosing the clock broke, exposing its face and hands to the outside. Soon a man who passed by the clock to check his watch noticed that the two timepieces indicated differing times. "Well, that's not right," he said, and he reached into the clock's broken housing to adjust the time to match his own watch.

A couple of hours later, somebody else walked by, looked at the clock, and said, "Would you look at that? Our clock has gotten behind. Maybe it's the night air." So he stopped to readjust the time to what he thought was correct.

You can see what's coming, can't you? Soon the clock lost all authority and "the correct time" became what anyone thought it should be.

In a similar way, when you abandon the Word of God as your final authority, the church begins to suffer just as that clock (and the townspeople) did. When you start to make church whatever you want it to be, rather than what God wants it to be, you lose all authority. You start to look more like the Book of Judges than the Book of Acts:

> **Judges:** "*Everyone did what was right in his own eyes*" (17:6); "*The children of Israel did evil in the sight of the LORD*" (2:11).
>
> **Acts:** "*They continued steadfastly in the apostles' doctrine and fellowship*" (2:42); "*And the Lord added to the church daily those who were being saved*" (2:47).

That's why Paul sounds so adamant when he says to Timothy, "*Preach the Word! Be ready in season and out of season. Convince, rebuke, exhort, with all longsuffering and teaching*" (2 Timothy 4:2). And that is why, for a pastor, every other activity in church life must take a backseat to the preaching of the Word of God.

Remember the account in Acts 6 when a crisis arose over meeting the physical needs of the church's members? The congregation presented the problem to the apostles, and they replied, "*It is not desirable that we should leave the word of God and serve tables*" (Acts 6:2). They instructed their friends to find people in the church whom God had gifted to take care of such needs, so that "*we will give ourselves continually to prayer and to the ministry of the word*" (v. 4).

That's the only way to build a thriving church.

I recently got a phone call from a pastor in Ohio who said he listened to our radio show every day. "You know," he said, "I listen and I'm intrigued because you're taking people through the Bible. *I'd* like to do that."

"Great," I said. "So do it!"

"Well, I can't," he replied sadly. "I want to. I know how to. But I can't."

"Why not?" I asked.

He paused and then said quietly, "I happen to be in a church that is based on a 'seeker friendly' model. My leadership board won't let me teach the Bible. They would have a fit if I did."

"Then you're in a dilemma," I replied, "because either you're going to have to get a new leadership board, or they're going to have to get a new pastor who will dance to their tune. But if you want to do what God wants you to do, then I say, 'just do it and let the chips fall where they may.' Only make sure you keep the priorities that God wants you to keep."

Result: A Blockbuster Pair

When we decide to radiate the glory of God and when we choose to reveal the truth of God, those two decisions are going to produce a pair of tremendous results. Look at John 17:13:

> *But now I come to You, and these things I speak in the world, that they may have My joy fulfilled in themselves.*

When you decide to give the glory of God and the Word of God their proper place, you reap both *joy* and *holiness.*

One of the things I most appreciate about the congregation I serve is that at the end of each Sunday service, everybody in church gets happy. They all clap! It might seem a little strange to outsiders, but I love it. Our people have an infectious joy that comes from the Word and from God-focused worship. These priorities produce a sense of godly euphoria. The world might look at us and say, "You're a bunch of fanatics!"—but oh, am I glad to serve among such fanatics!

I enjoy watching the World Series, but I'm no fanatic about it. I observe people in the crowds and see them jumping up and down and shouting and carrying on, and I think, *And they call us fanatics!* A ball gets hit out of the park, and they go crazy to the point of suffering a heart attack—and they call us fanatics when we exhibit the joy of the Lord?

We want to be those kinds of fanatics!

Psalm 119:1-2, 35 says, "*Happy are people of integrity who follow the law of the LORD, happy are those who obey His decrees and search for Him with all their hearts. . . . Make me walk along the path of Your commands, for that is where my happiness is found*" (NLT). The twin decisions to glorify God and to reveal His Word through your church life inevitably produce joy.

They also do something else—they produce holiness. "*I do not pray that You should take them out of the world,*"

Jesus prays, "*but that You should keep them from the evil one. They are not of the world, just as I am not of the world. Sanctify them . . .* " (vv. 15-17). The word translated "sanctify" is the Greek term *hagiazo*, which means "to be set apart." Jesus is praying for His disciples, "Make them wholly devoted to You, Lord." That's holiness.

And just how does Jesus ask His Father to sanctify His disciples? "*Sanctify them by Your truth,*" He prays. "*Your word is truth. As You sent Me into the world, I also have sent them into the world. And for their sakes I sanctify Myself, that they also may be sanctified by the truth*" (vv. 17-19). Jesus means that although the world is full of evil and deception, when you and I stick to revealing the truth of God by holding forth the Word of God, He'll keep us pure in the midst of this evil world.

If you're in the world but not in the Word, then very quickly you'll become of the world. On the other hand, if you're only in the Word all day but never in the world, then soon you'll become irrelevant to it. So we need to be in the Word, striving to understand God's principles, and then move about in the world so that we can influence the people around us for Jesus Christ.

The Psalmist said, "*Your word I have hidden in my heart, that I might not sin against You*" (Psalm 119:11). That's why our church emphasizes the teaching of the Word at every church-sponsored gathering. When we get together for a men's breakfast, everyone knows we're going to have a Bible study. When we meet for a small group, we expect to hear something from the Word. When our women gather, they look forward to a meeting based around Scripture. It's *all* going to revolve around the Word of God.

The Power of His Word

I am so glad for what the Word of God can do in my life! For years, people have come to me after a sermon and said, "Wow, that was exactly what I needed. Who told you about me?" or, "Honestly, were you following me this week, pastor?"

That's not me; that's the power of the Word of God.

The Holy Spirit knows exactly where and how to use the Word to bring correction, to supply encouragement, to give direction, and to get us moving in a positive direction.

> *"The word of God is living and powerful,"* says the writer to the Hebrews, *"and sharper than any two-edged sword, piercing even to the division of soul and spirit, and of joints and marrow, and is a discerner of the thoughts and intents of the heart"* (4:12).

Let's never allow our church to become the dreary place described by Natalie—a cold, uncaring, and irrelevant thing that prompts others to say, "Jesus, yes. Church, no."

And how do we steer clear of such a sad scene? The wonderful news is that when we worship God supremely and study His truth diligently, that's one tragedy we won't ever have to experience firsthand.

CHAPTER 3

A Place of Rescue

AND LOVE

A New York businessman once visited Chicago. While returning to his hotel after dinner, he noticed a sign that read, "Chinese Laundry." Since he had a bunch of dirty clothes piling up in his hotel room, he kept a careful mental note of the place. The next day he brought several bags of soiled shirts and pants and other apparel into the establishment and set them down on the counter.

The attendant looked at him quizzically, as if to say, "What is *this*?" When the businessman said nothing, the attendant asked him, "What are you doing?"

"This is my laundry," the businessman said. "I've always heard that Chinese laundries are amazing, so when I saw your sign, I decided to come here to get my laundry done."

The man behind the counter shook his head and said, "This isn't a laundry. It's a sign shop! You saw the sign 'Chinese Laundry,' but look around—there are lots of other signs, as well. You see them on the wall, on the floor, and in the window."

Sure enough, the businessman spotted signs for restaurants, for convenience stores, for piano tuners, and for a host of other establishments. He had taken his dirty laundry to the wrong place!

The Church can make a similar mistake. We, too, can send out false signals. Maybe we put up a sign that proclaims we're a church, or we erect a large cross, and soon people start bringing in their dirty laundry and broken lives. Sadly, we're sometimes so ill equipped to deal with the mess that we say, through our actions or our words, "We're so sorry, but you've come to the wrong place." And so these hurting people pick up their bags and look elsewhere for help.

Is that what the Church is supposed to be? Is that our purpose? In His amazing prayer of John 17, Jesus makes it clear that the Church really is supposed to be a place that deals effectively and compassionately with the dirty laundry, broken lives, and soiled backgrounds of the hurting people who come to us.

Rescue the Enemies of God

As Jesus prepared to leave this Earth and return to Heaven, He prayed for those He was about to leave behind. We know they heard His prayer, or, otherwise, we would have no record of His words. Let's return to John 17 and listen to His petition:

> *I have given them Your word; and the world has hated them because they are not of the world, just as I am not of the world. I do not pray that You should take them out of the world, but that You should keep them from the evil one. They are not of the world, just as I am not of the world. Sanctify them by Your truth. Your word is truth. As You sent Me into the world, I also have sent them into the world.* (vv. 14-18)

You probably know that God "called" you into His family and into His service, but did you realize that He also "sent" you into the world to accomplish His purposes? You have a job to do; you are on a mission from God, a rescue operation.

Jesus did not design the Church to become a "bless me" club. He didn't intend it as a place where we come merely to feel good about ourselves and to get some good pampering (though we *should* feel good when we gather with God's people and God *does* love to lavish His grace upon us). The Church exists not only to radiate God's glory, not only to reveal His truth, but also to rescue His enemies—those who at this moment are in deadly opposition to God because of their sin.

Somebody once said, "The church is the only society on earth that exists for the benefit of non-members." I like that! We exist for the benefit of those who are not yet in the Church. Jesus taught His disciples to focus not merely on themselves, but to *"lift up your eyes and look at the fields, for they are already white for harvest!"* (John 4:35). Jesus wasn't talking about a crop of wheat or barley, but about a crop of needy people who lacked a saving relationship with God. In this particular case, He was referring to the men and women of Samaria, a town of "half-breeds" whom most Jews detested.

Notice that He called the harvest "white." In other words, the people were ready to be picked; they were ripe to be rescued. The Samaritans had seen the remarkable work that Jesus had done in the life of one of their marriage-challenged citizens, and they had come out to see for themselves if He could do some similar work in their own ravaged hearts.

Sometimes I think of that verse when I'm in a mall and see hundreds of people, just waiting to be rescued. The field is white for harvest! Or when I drive on some busy freeway,

I see people honking and shouting and cursing (or maybe shaving and eating and applying lipstick). It's easy to get annoyed and think, *What are all these people doing on my road? I've got somewhere to go, and they're making it difficult for me!* Jesus would say, "Lift up your eyes—they're ready for harvest!"

So often, our churches turn inward rather than outward. Church becomes all about us and our comfort rather than the hurting world and its need for a Savior. We must remember that Jesus said to His disciples, "Go into all the world." Somehow we changed His mandate from a "go" into a "come." While Jesus told us to "Go," we tell the world, "Come." And then maybe we add, "If you can find us, we'll tell you the truth."

But "Come" is not the same as "Go."

Saved, Serving, Sent

The Bible reveals a healthy pattern of Christian growth that you could summarize like this: *saved, serving, sent*. I think that's the normal pattern for every believer in Christ.

When God saves us, we get excited. We enjoy the benefits of salvation and discover how great it can be to get into the Word. It feels wonderful to meet people who share our new life in Christ and to discover with them all the love God has for us. It's energizing to learn of all the great things He has in store for His people.

However, after a while, we become just a little bored with having someone feed us all the time. We want to discover our own spiritual gifts and get involved in our local church and begin serving the Lord in some capacity. We want to give out, not just take in.

So we begin taking note of the world around us. As we do, we start to think, *You know, they need this. They need God's family, too. They need to belong to Him, as well. They also need salvation!* That thought takes us out of our own little world, and soon we discover that our Father has a much bigger plan for us than merely focusing on ourselves.

One author put it this way: "Christian maturity is being a responsible son or daughter of God." [1] Who are the mature in Christ? They are believers who have stopped being concerned solely about their own needs and pursuits. These mature Christians have enthusiastically entered into the global vision of their Father. They are the ones who partner with God to accomplish the aims of the Lord's Prayer: "*Your kingdom come. Your will be done on earth as it is in heaven*" (Matthew 6:10).

It's like a son who's being groomed to take over the family business. Instead of racing fast cars and running around with girls, he finally buckles down and says "Dad, I'm a part of it now. It's my business too, and I'm going to work hard and undertake the burden of this company."

And what is the family business of the Church? It's to partner with God in rescuing His enemies. Jesus said it best: "Father, as You sent me into the world, so I send them into the world."

Okay, but How?

God has called us to help Him rescue those who are at odds with Him and His ways. Okay...but how are we supposed to do that?

1. See Endnotes, page 247.

As you might expect, Jesus does not leave us in the dark. In His prayer of John 17, He gives us three ways to partner with God in Heaven's ongoing rescue operation. We help in this mission of rescue by...

...knowing something;

...growing in something;

...and going.

First, we have to *know our position in Christ*. Jesus says of His disciples, "*They are not of the world, just as I am not of the world. Sanctify them by Your truth. Your word is truth. As You sent Me into the world, I also have sent them into the world*" (vv.16-18). We are not of the world, Jesus says, but we are sent out into it.

Jesus says we are "in" the world but not "of" it. And what was Jesus' relationship to the world? We find the answer in verses 3 and 4: "*And this is eternal life, that they may know You, the only true God, and Jesus Christ whom You have sent. I have glorified You on the earth. I have finished the work which You have given Me to do.*" Jesus saw the world as a stopping off point in which to do His Father's work. Once He had finished that, He was out of here. He was on the Earth—in the world to accomplish a specific task—but not of it.

It's the same with us.

Why Such a Preoccupation?

So why is it that, if we know this world is so very temporary, we become so preoccupied with it?

Imagine you were in a waiting area at an airport. You're fully aware that you'll be there for only two hours as you wait to switch airplanes—but yet you spend all of your energy redecorating the airport bathroom.

"Why are you doing this?" a friend asks. "You're going to be here only for a little while, and then you're out of here. What's the point?"

"Oh, I know," you say, "but I want my bathroom here to look *really* nice."

It's a lame idea. Nineteenth century American evangelist Dwight L. Moody used to say that the church of his day reminded him of firemen straightening out pictures on the wall of a burning house.

Think of an astronaut. Outer space is simply not his element. He needs a space suit to survive in it, because he's not designed to live in the vacuum and cold of space. For him to survive "in" it, he has to depend on specialized equipment.

Or think of a scuba diver. The water isn't his element. He is not "of " the water, so in order to survive "in" it, he needs special gear.

We are in the same position, spiritually, in this world. Unless we know our true position with this world—in it and not of it—we're going to drown. Do you know why? Because in verse 14 Jesus says, *"The world has hated them because they are not of the world."* An occupational hazard of following Jesus Christ is that people are going to treat you based on their view of God. If they don't like the God you represent, they're not going to like you.

Second, we have to be *growing in preparation.* That takes us to verse 17: *"Sanctify them* [or set them apart, make them holy] *by Your truth; Your word is truth."* We have to be prepared to handle whatever comes to us through the Word of God. Peter wrote, *"As newborn babes, desire* [or crave] *the pure milk of the word, that you may grow thereby"* (1 Peter 2:2).

Why is familiarity with the Bible, and the ability to handle it well, a prerequisite to spiritual growth? Here's why: To swim in a sea of worldly temptations, you need your scuba gear. For you to survive, you need the right gear. You must counteract the pressure to conform from the outside with an equal pressure to resist from the inside. If not, you'll fall to it.

And the world *constantly* pressures us! God warns us and encourages us not to conform to it (see Romans 12:2). So we need a great pressure from the inside—the Holy Spirit living within us—in order to resist it.

An acquaintance of mine, a pastor in the Los Angeles area, once received a letter from a radio listener who was looking for Bible study helps. He wanted to learn how he could receive Bible study cassettes of this guy's sermons. Listen to his request for help:

> *Please send me some ammunition. The battle lines are drawn, the trenches are being dug, and I'm not one of those to be caught shamefaced when our Commanding Officer returns. When the record is being reviewed, I want it written that the soldier in question, namely me, after repeatedly disobeying orders and going AWOL during wartime alert, finally donned his armor, reported back to his Commanding Officer, fought courageously and fearlessly (without batting an eye), hit the enemy with everything he could get his hands on, and inflicted heavy damage in strategic areas—to the credit of his patient, forgiving, loving Commanding Officer.*

One concept in this letter applies equally to all of us: "I want it to be said that he took everything he could get his hands on to inflict damage on the enemy." By knowing our position in the world and by growing in preparation for the battle ahead—by grabbing all the equipment we need to help rescue the enemies of God—we become the kind of Church Jesus wants us to be.

Third, we have to *go out and fulfill the mandate.* Jesus prayed, *"As You sent Me into the world, I also have sent them into the world"* (v. 18). The purpose of our "knowing" and "growing" is not so that we can keep "sitting," but that we might effectively go into all the world to preach the gospel to every creature (see Mark 16:15).

A Place to Belong

Everyone suffers from faulty concepts of what the Church is to be and do. The most common is to see the church as a specific place where people meet, rather than as a group of people who meet at a place. This is more than just semantics! There is a big difference between the two.

If we see the church as a place where people meet, then we'll constantly be on the lookout for the kind of place that most suits us. We'll visit here and go there and hop over somewhere else, never "landing" anywhere. But if we see the church as a group of people whom Christ has selected out of the world, who meet at some designated place to grow in grace and glorify God, then we'll continually evaluate what kind of people we are to become for the glory of God.

Christ calls us not only to be believers but also belongers. We are to belong to a specific, local group of people who look for ways to grow spiritually and to reach out to the world in love. We're not just believers but belongers together—even if we look very different from one another.

Your congregation needs you the whole year around, not just sitting in the pews, but as an active part of Jesus' Bride, the Church. It needs your help in God's ongoing rescue operation. It needs your help as a loving member of a unified Body of Christ.

In short, it needs you if it is to become what Jesus has called it to become.

CHAPTER 4

You've Come to Church—

NOW WHAT?

I gave my life to Jesus Christ in 1973 after watching a Billy Graham crusade on television. As Billy turned toward the camera, he said, "If you're watching by television, you can know Christ." Right then, I prayed to receive Christ. At the end of his broadcast, Billy said (as he usually did), "And make sure that you go to church next Sunday." Rev. Graham always made regular church attendance an important part of his message.

Unfortunately, many of us have all sorts of creative reasons (also known as excuses) why we can't come to church. Anticipating this, one creative church put the following announcement in its Sunday bulletin:

> *To make it possible for everyone to attend church next Sunday, we're going to have a special "No Excuse Sunday." Cots will be placed in the foyer for those who say, "Sunday is my only day to sleep in." Murine will be available for those with tired eyes from staying up too late watching TV on Saturday night. We will have steel helmets for those who say, "The roof would cave in if I ever came to church." Blankets will be provided for those who think the*

> *church is too cold and we will have fans for those who think the church is too hot. We will have hearing aides for those who say the pastor speaks too softly and cotton for those who say he preaches too loudly. Scorecards will be available for those who wish to list the hypocrites present. Some relatives will be in attendance for those who like to go visiting on Sunday. There will be 100 TV dinners for those who can't go to church and also cook dinner. One section will be devoted to trees and grass for those who like to seek God in nature. And finally, the sanctuary will be decorated with both Christmas poinsettias and Easter lilies for those who have never seen church without them.* [1]

Another time, I heard about a guy who was very late for his foursome's tee time on Sunday morning. His fellow golfers were about to go out without him when he finally arrived.

> "Sorry I'm late, guys," he said. "But this morning I had to toss a coin to see whether I should play golf or go to church, per an agreement I made with my wife. Heads, I'd play golf; tails, I'd go to church. Guys—it probably took me *forty to forty-five* tosses before I got heads!"

Good Counsel From an Unexpected Source

It seems strange to look in the Old Testament for good counsel about how to approach church, but that's exactly what we find in Ecclesiastes 5. "Skip," you might say, "why would you choose an Old Testament passage to discuss a New Testament topic like the church?"

---

1. See Endnotes, page 247.

If you look at the opening words of Ecclesiastes, you might change your opinion: *"The words of the Preacher, the son of David, king in Jerusalem."* The word "preacher" in Hebrew is *qoheleth*, which means "one who assembles, a caller, a congregator." The corresponding Greek term is *ecclesiastes*.

In the Book of Ecclesiastes, Solomon wanted to call together various philosophies of life to judge their effectiveness. He got all sorts of ideas, ideologies, and approaches together to determine the best and most fulfilling way to live. In the course of his investigation he made several sharp observations about the way people lived back then—and still live today.

One phrase keeps popping up in his book: "Life under the sun." After every observation Solomon makes, he comes to the same conclusion: "Vanity of vanities, all is vanity." No matter what experience he has—pleasure, wealth, friendships—he finds everything empty in the end. "Life under the sun" is meaningless, he says.

By the time he gets to chapter 5, Solomon turns to the Temple that he built. I picture him standing outside of the gate, maybe incognito with a robe around him, watching the people come to the Temple, bringing their sacrifices, singing their songs, and saying their liturgy. He carefully observes the people's religious practices. I can envision him saying, "Okay, so you've come to church—*now* what?"

As we consider the first seven verses of Ecclesiastes 5, we will ask three questions:

1. What is your approach to God?
2. What is your commitment to God?
3. What is your attitude toward God?

Notice what Solomon had to say about all three questions in Ecclesiastes 5:1-7:

> *Walk prudently when you go to the house of God; and draw near to hear rather than to give the sacrifice of fools, for they do not know that they do evil.*
>
> *Do not be rash with your mouth, and let not your heart utter anything hastily before God. For God is in heaven, and you on earth; therefore let your words be few. For a dream comes through much activity, and a fool's voice is known by his many words. When you make a vow to God, do not delay to pay it; for He has no pleasure in fools. Pay what you have vowed— better not to vow than to vow and not pay.*
>
> *Do not let your mouth cause your flesh to sin, nor say before the messenger of God* [that is, the preacher] *that it was an error. Why should God be angry at your excuse and destroy the work of your hands? For in the multitude of dreams and many words there is also vanity. But fear God.*

What Is Your Approach to God?

Solomon identified three primary ways by which the people of his day tried to approach God. Each had varying degrees of effectiveness.

1. The Ceremonial Approach

If you know anything about the Old Testament Temple in Jerusalem, you recognize that the centerpiece of Jewish religious life was the regalia and ritual of the ceremony. It was all about bringing sacrifices and having priests officiating in a certain way, in a certain manner, and at a certain time. It was all about the ceremony. In verse 1, however, God, through Solomon, refers to "the sacrifice of fools."

"Wait a minute!" you say, "I thought *God* prescribed all of the sacrifices. I thought they were *His* idea. But if that's true, then why would Solomon refer to them as 'the sacrifice of fools'?" He did so because he observed many people coming to the Temple in a *purely* ceremonial way. They meticulously kept the ceremonial law—"this animal, not that one; slaughter it in this way, not that way"—even as they broke the moral law. Solomon observed them worshiping idols, slandering each other, harboring bitterness, refusing to forgive, stealing from each other—all while saying, "But we're coming to the Temple and offering our sacrifices in the proper way. We're good!"—as they pat one another on the back.

Repeatedly through the Old Testament prophets, God indicted His people for this very behavior. In the opening chapter of Isaiah, God says, *"I am sick of your sacrifices... Don't bring me any more burnt offerings! I don't want the fat from your rams or other animals. I don't want to see the blood from your offerings of bulls and rams and goats. The incense you bring me is a stench in my nostrils! Your celebrations of the new moon and the Sabbath day, and your special days for fasting—even your most pious meetings—are all sinful and false. I want nothing more to do with them"* (vv. 11, 13, NLT).

Many times we approach God thinking that our religious ceremony can substitute for our obedience. "So long as I go to church (or have been baptized or been confirmed or participated in this or that ritual or take Communion), I'm covered." We think it's all about the ceremony.

Remember Cain and Abel? One was a farmer, the other a shepherd. One brought a sacrifice to God of the fruit of the ground. That was Cain. And then his brother brought the firstlings of his flock. The Bible says that God respected the offering of Abel but did not respect the offering of Cain—

and that bummed out Cain. Your Bible probably doesn't say, "bummed out"; that's the NSV (the New Skip Version). It actually says, "His countenance had fallen." Loose translation: He was bummed out!

God came to him and said, "Cain, why art thou bummed out?" And then the Lord said, "If you did right, would you not be accepted?"

Did you get that? "If you did right, you'd be accepted." The problem wasn't the particular sacrifice Cain brought, but his attitude and behavior in bringing it. His life wasn't right. So God was saying to him, "Cain, I'm looking beyond the ceremony into the heart—and what I see in your life isn't right. If you were right, you'd be accepted; but you're not right."

That's the problem with a purely ceremonial approach.

Cain stands in a long line of people who struggled with this. Saul, the first king of Israel, had the same flawed mentality. At one point God instructed him to fight and completely destroy both the Amalekites and their possessions. But Saul disobeyed God and spared some of the best animals of his enemy. When the prophet Samuel heard and saw what Saul was bringing back with him, he said, "Why didn't you do what God told you to do? Why didn't you destroy everything like God instructed you?" The king replied, "Oh, I brought back the best of these animals to sacrifice to the Lord." But Samuel answered, *"Has the Lord as great delight in burnt offerings and sacrifices, as in obeying the voice of the Lord? Behold, to obey is better than sacrifice, and to heed than the fat of rams"* (1 Samuel 15:22; see 1 Samuel 15:1-23 for full story).

The king thought his ceremony could substitute for his obedience—but it couldn't. God flatly rejected his sacrifice.

In the same way, if you go to church thinking, *I'm making God really happy by showing up today. So long as I go through the ceremony, I'm good with God,* then you're sorely mistaken. That's merely a ceremonial approach—and God will *never* accept it.

Years ago our church needed a building—and we could not afford one. An owner of a suitable facility heard of our need and decided to rent us his building for what we could afford. I saw this as a direct gift from God. As I was about to sign the lease, the guy leaned over his desk and said, "You know, the way I figure it, Skip, this is going to be enough to push me over into Heaven on judgment day."

I dropped the pen.

If ever there were a time when I *didn't* want to preach the gospel, that was it. I thought that if I spoke the truth, I could lose the deal. But I said to the man, "There's Heaven and there's hell, and you are not on your way to Heaven. And you can't get there by thinking that you can do something to earn God's favor. God loves you and God will receive you, but you can't do this thinking that God will say, 'Okay, you've done the ceremony; you made Skip a good deal. Come on in!'" I carefully explained the gospel to him—and, praise God, we still got the deal.

2. *The Superficial Approach*

Ecclesiastes 5:2-3 describes the second approach:

> *Do not be rash with your mouth, and let not your heart utter anything hastily before God. For God is in heaven, and you on earth; therefore let your words be few. For a dream comes through much activity, and a fool's voice is known by his many words.*

Maybe you ramble quickly through a prayer list—that's "rash" speech—and then think, *I'm gonna speak lots of flowery words and say some eloquent prayers*—that's "much" speech. Yet it is possible to pray a lot, using many elegant words, and yet never connect with God in prayer.

Jesus once told a story about two people who went up to the Temple to pray. One was a Pharisee, the other a tax collector. Jesus said, "*The Pharisee stood and prayed thus with himself, 'God, I thank You that I am not like other men*'" (Luke 18:11). In other words, the Pharisee wasn't praying to God at all; he was praying "with himself," that is, for his own benefit. Thus he spoke only to himself. He probably stood in the Temple, raised his head, and prayed out loud, all the while thinking, *Man, I'm really good! I can pray! I'm eloquent!* It was all superficial; only for show.

This is why Jesus said, "*When you pray, do not use vain repetitions as the heathen do*" (Matthew 6:7). Ancient pagans had a habit of repeating certain "magical" phrases over and over again, thinking that the longer they did so, the more the gods would hear them. Jesus said, "Don't do that."

Remember the story of the prophet Elijah on Mount Carmel in which he had a famous contest with the prophets of Baal? Elijah probably uttered no more than twenty words, but the Bible says that the false prophets prayed from morning until midday (see 1 Kings 18). They prayed for hours straight, repeating the same mantra, shouting the same words. But nothing happened.

Why not? Because there is only one God, and they weren't praying to Him. They thought they would be heard because of their many loud prayers, but they were not.

Solomon observed that many people came to the Temple superficially. Long ago he discovered what one group of researchers recently learned when they took a look at "church-going" America. We've all heard the statistics that insist most Americans claim to be born-again Christians.

"Yeah, I believe in God. I'm a Christian." This group decided to examine the people who call themselves Christians. It observed not only their church attendance but also four key areas of their personal lives. Their research revealed that 19 percent of Americans really are committed; they regularly practice what they say they believe. Another 22 percent are what the study called "modestly religious," and 29 percent were "barely" or "nominally religious." [2]

Things haven't changed much over the centuries, have they?

3. *The Thoughtful Approach*

Look again at Ecclesiastes 5:1: "*Walk prudently* [thoughtfully, carefully] *when you go to the house of God; and draw near to hear rather than to give the sacrifice of fools, for they do not know that they do evil.*"

The King James Version translates the phrase, "walk prudently," as "keep thy foot." In other words, "Watch thy step!" Be very thoughtful and careful when you come to church. Be prepared.

How often do you come to church prepared?

"Don't you just throw on a coat, put your hair back, put pants and shoes on, apply a little makeup, head out the door, and you're set? That's being prepared." Yes, that's outward preparation—but do you ever prepare inwardly? How about saying, "Lord, I'm about to go to church. I'm going to meet with people I know and meet others I've never met. First and foremost, I am going to meet with You, because it's Your house. It's about You! I want to walk very carefully and get my heart prepared before I make this journey."

God's Word says, "Walk prudently when you go to the house of God; and draw near to hear rather than to give

[2] See Endnotes, page 248.

the sacrifice of fools." *This* is why we come prepared. We ought to approach God prudently and thoughtfully and carefully—because God promises to speak to us. It's like the young Samuel who said, *"Speak, for Your servant hears"* (1 Samuel 3:10). God *will* speak to your heart.

The New Living Translation says, "As you enter the house of God, keep your ears open and your mouth shut." That's very clear, isn't it? As someone reminded us years ago, God gave us two ears and one mouth for a reason. We should listen twice as much as we talk. When we come into the house of God, we need to keep our ears wide open to hear whatever God has to say to us.

The best worship comes when we listen first. Anointed speakers need anointed listeners. Walt Whitman, one of America's great poets, once said, "To have great poets, there must be great audiences."

Nehemiah 8 is a preacher's dream. The Jewish exiles have returned from Babylon to Jerusalem, Ezra is there, and they all get their Bibles out (in their case, their Torah scrolls):

> *Now all the people gathered together as one man in the open square that was in front of the Water Gate; and they told Ezra the scribe to bring the Book of the Law of Moses, which the Lord had commanded Israel. So Ezra the priest brought the Law before the assembly of men and women and all who could hear with understanding on the first day of the seventh month. Then he read from it in the open square that was in front of the Water Gate from morning until midday.* (vv. 1-3)

That's a *long* church service, with a Bible reading that probably lasted four hours! How many of us today could take *that?* And by the way, they didn't sit; they stood the whole time.

When I first visited India, I felt so impressed with the believers there. They walked for hours to reach our meeting place, and once they had come to church, they *wanted* a four-hour service. I thought I could get by with a one-hour message. When I finished, I thought, *Whew, I'm done.*

"Oh no," they said, "not so fast! We're just starting." They wanted me to keep going...and going...and going. That is the idea in Nehemiah 8:

> *Then he read from it in the open square . . . before the men and women and those who could understand; and the ears of all the people were attentive to the Book of the Law. So Ezra the scribe stood on a platform of wood which they had made for the purpose; and beside him* [stood all kinds of people with funny names]. *And Ezra opened the book in the sight of all the people, for he was standing above all the people; and when he opened it, all the people stood up. And Ezra blessed the LORD, the great God. Then all the people answered, "Amen, Amen!"* [an interactive, participative Bible study] *while lifting up their hands. And they bowed their heads and worshiped the LORD with their faces to the ground.* (vv. 3-6)

That was anointed listening! The people worshiped God as He spoke to them from His Word. Somebody might say, "Yeah, but God doesn't speak like He used to." Instead, I think the problem is that people don't listen. I believe God is speaking to us all the time, but He has to compete today with hundreds of other speakers who want to crowd out His voice.

What Is Your Commitment to God?

Solomon speaks about making commitments to God in Ecclesiastes 5:4-7:

> *When you make a vow to God, do not delay to pay it; for He has no pleasure in fools. Pay what you have vowed—better not to vow than to vow and not pay. Do not let your mouth cause your flesh to sin, nor say before the messenger of God that it was an error. Why should God be angry at your excuse and destroy the work of your hands? For in the multitude of dreams and many words there is also vanity. But fear God.*

The setting is the Hebrew Temple as the people bring their sacrifices for worship. Some of those who come make some kind of promise or commitment or vow to the Lord.

In Deuteronomy 23 and Numbers 30, the law makes provision for making a vow—a public affirmation of what someone intends to do for the Lord. No one had to make such a vow. God never made it compulsory; it was always voluntary. But God said, "Once you do make the vow, be sure to keep it. Make good on it."

So often we make vows to God when we find ourselves in the storms of life. Then in the calms of life, we break those vows. "Lord, if You'll just get me through this, I promise I'll . . . " and then we make some promise. God said, "If you vow it, make sure you keep it."

Worship should be a time to make commitments. Every time we gather and open our Bibles, we should concentrate on transformation, not on mere information. We have heard something from God; we have come to worship Him; we're singing songs and reading the Word—now what? What's next?

Solomon might say, "Make it a time of making a commitment based upon what you have heard." That's the scriptural pattern.

After Joshua gave his final speech to the people of Israel, he said, *"Choose for yourselves this day whom you will serve"* (Joshua 24:15). In other words, "It's time to make a commitment, folks."

Elijah did a very similar thing. After that memorable contest on Mount Carmel between the prophets of Baal and God, he said, *"How long will you falter between two opinions? If the LORD is God, follow Him; but if Baal, follow him"* (1 Kings 18:21). In other words, "Make a decision! Make a commitment! Make a choice!"

Jesus did this too. John 6 describes a hard message He preached that prompted many people to get up and walk out. He turned to His disciples and asked them for a commitment: "Will you also leave?" And Simon Peter replied, *"Lord, to whom shall we go? You have the words of eternal life"* (v. 68). In Caesarea Philippi, Jesus repeated His challenge for commitment, "I have a question for you. Who do people say that I am?"

"Oh, there are all sorts of opinions. Some think You're John the Baptist or Jeremiah or one of the prophets."

"But who do *you* say that I am?" (see Matthew 16:13-15). He brought His men to a point where they had to make a choice.

What choices have you made? What vows have you spoken? Maybe it was something like this: "Lord, I accept You into my heart as my Savior and my Master." How are you doing with that one? Is He still Master? Is He still Someone you pursue and seek and love and follow and obey?

Many of us once stood on a church platform and said to the person standing next to us, “For better, for worse, for richer or poorer, in sickness and in health, to love and to cherish until death [not “debt”] do us part.” How are you doing with that commitment?

Still others have made a commitment to a church: “I’m here; you can count on me! I’m going to serve. I love this body.” Those are all important and great commitments. How are you doing with them?

A young college guy once went into a photo studio with a framed picture of his girlfriend, looking to get a copy made. The shop owner told him, “I’m going to have to dismantle the frame and take out the glass to get to the photograph. That’s how I make copies.”

“Fair enough,” the young man said.

As the owner took apart the frame, he noticed a beautiful love note on the back of the photograph. “Dearest Tom,” it said, “I love you. I love you with all my heart. My love for you grows each day. I will love you forever and ever and ever. My heart is yours for all of eternity.” It was signed, “Diane.”

Then the man noticed a P.S. written below the lovely note: “P.S. — If we ever break up, I want this picture back.”

Is there a P.S. in your relationship with God?

“Oh yes, Lord, You’re my Master and Savior,” we say, “but here’s a contingency clause.” Is there some P.S. in the vows and commitments that you have made to Jesus? What is your commitment to Christ?

“Fine, then,” someone says. “The Bible tells me that I don’t have to say the vow; only that if I do say the vow, I have to do it. So I’m just going to sit in church, week after week, and not say any vows.” You could do that, of course; but if you do, recognize that you have just reduced yourself to one of the first two approaches. You're choosing either a ceremonial approach to God or a superficial approach to God. Such an approach is not careful, thoughtful, or authentic—and it won't bring you where you want to go.

What Is Your Attitude toward God?

Most of your approach and commitment to God depends upon your attitude toward God. And that's exactly what Solomon focuses on in verse 7: *"For in the multitude of dreams and many words there is also vanity. But fear God."* That's his conclusion.

And what does it mean to "fear God"? It doesn't mean that you have to be afraid of God, shaking in your boots that He might strike you down at any moment for the slightest infraction. The main idea is to have a reverential awe for a loving God, based on your loving and humble submission to Him. The phrase is found some fifty times in the Old Testament, so it must be very important.

"I reverence You, Lord. I love You. I respect You. I honor You as the Almighty Creator of the universe." This is the bottom line—"But fear God."

As we've worked our way through the first seven verses of Ecclesiastes 5, have you noticed a pattern in its wording? *"The house of God"* (v. 1), *"Your vows to God"* (v. 4), *"Fear God"* (v. 7). So what do you think is the key component in coming to church?

GOD! It's all about God.

One of my favorite worship songs says, "I'm coming back to the heart of worship, and it's all about You, Jesus."[3] I love

3. See Endnotes, page 248.

that! It's so rich and powerful. Truth be told, however, some of us can't honestly sing that lyric. If we were to sing the words honestly, it would come out, "I'm coming back to the heart of worship, because it's all about me." None of us would ever actually sing such a line, of course; but by the way we live and speak and interact, we've made it all about us.

Our world tells us to live for ourselves, yet we serve a God who says, "Make Me number one in your life. Fear Me; love Me; respect Me above everything else."

An advertisement in *Psychology Today* said, "I love me. I am not conceited. I'm just a good friend to myself, and I like to do whatever makes me feel good."[4] That's why, when we gather as the Church, we are making a statement which is *contra mundum*, "against the world." We don't adopt the world's value system. Church is *not* about us. It's about fearing, glorifying, and honoring God.

Never Let It Grow Stale

When you go to church, how do you approach God? Do you show up for worship with a deep commitment and a reverential spirit?

Let's encourage each other to come to church carefully and thoughtfully. One easy way to begin is to make it a habit to get to church on time. If the service starts at 9 a.m., then coming at 9:20 a.m. shows a lack of thought and care. Let's come with the attitude, "I want my first breath of worship to be thoughtful and careful, not rushed and frazzled and out of breath."

Second, let's make a commitment similar to the one made by the young boy Samuel: "Lord, I've come to hear. So speak,

---

4. See Endnotes, page 248.

Lord, for Your servant is listening. What do You want me to do?"

Last, let's come to God with a reverential attitude, not a casual or flippant spirit. Remember Solomon's instruction: "Fear God."

What is the one truth that you and I hear more than any other in our Christian experience? Without question, it's this: "Jesus died for your sins." We hear it every time we go to any Bible-preaching church. "Jesus died for you on the Cross." We hear it so often, in fact, that sometimes it goes right over our heads. The sentence becomes meaningless. Familiarity really can breed contempt! So let me give you three key suggestions on how to best approach God:

- *Guard yourself against formality.* It's so easy to fall into when we come to church: "It's just something we always do—nothing remarkable."
- *Devote yourself to consistency.* You may say, "Hey, I'm consistent! Every Christmas and Easter, I'm there." Work at your consistency in fellowship with other believers, in reading the Word, in loving God.
- *Let your relationship with God be your priority.* Let nothing else interfere. Make your relationship of love and intimacy with the Lord the most important thing in your life.

Have you ever suffered through the death of someone you loved deeply? If so, then you know deep pain. That death caused a major reaction in your heart—much like a boy who once lost his younger brother.

The boy's family lived way out in the country. A single, lonely road connected the family's house to the outside world and few cars ever used it. But one day, as the family's youngest son was out riding his bicycle, a car struck and killed him. His older brother wrote:

Later when my father picked up the mangled, twisted bike, I heard him sob out loud for the first time in my life. He carried it to the barn and placed it in a spot that we seldom used. My father's terrible sorrow has eased with the passing of time, but for many years whenever he saw that bike, tears began streaming down his face. Since then, I have often prayed, "Lord, keep the memory of Your death as fresh as *that* to me. Every time I partake of your memorial supper, let my heart be stirred, as though You died only yesterday. Never let the communion service become a mere formality for me, but always a tender and touching experience."[5]

When we approach God like that, we will never have to worry about our relationship with Him going stale.

5. See Endnotes, page 248.

CHAPTER 5

Why Can't We All

JUST GET ALONG?

Southern California family, I can tell you that my brothers and I did not always get along. We argued, we competed, and we fought pretty hard.

You have to pity my mom. No girls, just four boys!

One time I found a knife in the road. When I showed it to one brother, he said, "Oh, you think you're pretty hot!"

"Well," I said, "I could take *you*!"

We immediately got into a fight. I stabbed him in the arm with the knife; he responded by picking up a pencil and stabbing me in my arm.

Another time, while my parents were away enjoying a rare date night together, I threw one of my brothers through the front window of our house. He landed in the front lawn. When they returned home later that night, we found ourselves in *big* trouble.

Understandably upset, they fixed the window that very week. And the following week, my brother threw me through the same window.

That's just a little snapshot of us growing up!

I have to say, it's not much different in the Christian family. We have all sorts of characters among us: spiritual babes in Christ, adolescents in the Lord, spiritually mature men and women. But regardless of our level of maturity, we don't always get along. Friction exists even within the Christian family.

I heard recently about a dad relaxing at home, reading the newspaper. His daughter and her friends were playing in the next room. Gradually their little voices got increasingly louder and rowdier. They started arguing, then pushing and shoving one another, then calling each other names. Finally the dad shouted, "You girls *stop* it!" The commotion halted immediately. And then, very innocently and sweetly, his daughter answered, "It's okay, Daddy. We're just playing church."

It's Never Been Easy

Getting along as Christians has never been easy. Think of the twelve apostles; did they always get along? Hardly! Sometimes they argued over who would be the greatest in the kingdom. Other times they argued over who would sit at Jesus' right hand, which was the place of privilege. Constant friction seemed to shake their little group.

Many years after Jesus' death and resurrection, the Book of Acts describes a church-wide council at Jerusalem that met to settle a sharp dispute over what constituted salvation.

More than once, Peter and Paul argued over how best to deal with Gentiles— should they be treated just like Jews?

Even Paul and Barnabas, after working so well together on a difficult missionary assignment, got into such a heated argument that they parted company. Thereafter, they went in two opposite directions in ministry.

And it doesn't get any better when you look into extra-biblical history. There you'll read of inquisitions and crusades, councils and denominations, lawsuits and bitter rivalries. In a report published more than a decade ago, *U.S. News and World Report* counted at least 22,000 separate Christian denominations and sects worldwide.[1]

And yet Jesus told us quite plainly, *"By this all will know that you are My disciples, if you have love for one another"* (John 13:35).

How can we learn to get along in the family of God? What biblical principles can help us grow the kind of love for our fellow believers that Jesus insists we must all demonstrate? Philippians 2:1-4 gives us a great place to start.

A Little Background

Paul wrote his letter to the Philippian church from jail. The Philippians had become great friends of his and Paul loved them deeply. Still, this church faced some enormous pressures, both from the outside and from the inside.

From the outside they had to deal with the pressure of false teachers who were trying to infiltrate the church. And from the inside they had to contend with fighting church members who threatened to fracture the harmony of the congregation. These twin pressures prompted Paul to write in Philippians 3, *"Finally, my brethren, rejoice in the Lord. For me to write the same things to you is not tedious, but for you it is safe. Beware of dogs"*—and he doesn't mean poodles or Afghans or the furry little barking creatures you might have at your house, but a group of people he's about to name—*"beware of evil workers, beware of the*

1. See Endnotes, page 248.

mutilation!" (vv. 1-2). Paul had in mind a pack of legalistic teachers from the outside who were trying to convince the Philippians that they had to perform certain rituals in order to be saved. These false prophets stirred up a lot of trouble from the outside.

And then in chapter 4 the apostle writes, *"Therefore, my beloved and longed-for brethren, my joy and crown, so stand fast in the Lord, beloved. I implore Euodia and I implore Syntyche to be of the same mind in the Lord. And I urge you also, true companion, help these women who labored with me in the gospel"* (vv. 1-3). Here Paul mentions a pair of women in the church who stirred division when they insisted on two contrasting ways of getting something done.

These two stresses—one from the outside and one from the inside—put the church under tremendous pressure. They pitted church member against church member and made it difficult for the congregation to get along. And yet Paul insisted that they *had* to get along—and so he gave them some important principles to help them mend fences and get back to loving one another, as Jesus had commanded them.

Redeemed but Imperfect

Have you noticed that your own church is far from a group of perfect people? How could you not notice it? In fact, it is a group of redeemed-yet-imperfect believers. Probably you've heard this saying a million times, but it bears repeating: "If you ever find a perfect church, *don't join it!* Because you'll ruin it."

The Church is filled with redeemed, imperfect people. And yet God calls us to be a part of it. When Jesus stood in the synagogue at Nazareth, His hometown, He read from the prophet Isaiah. *"The Spirit of the LORD is upon Me,"* He declared, *"because He has anointed Me to preach the gospel to the poor; He has sent Me to heal the brokenhearted, to proclaim liberty to the captives and recovery of sight to the blind, to set at liberty those who are oppressed"* (Luke 4:18). Luke says that Jesus then closed the scroll, handed it back to the attendant, sat down, and announced, *"Today this Scripture is fulfilled in your hearing"* (v. 21).

Now, did you catch what kind of people Jesus came to help and to save? He calls them "poor" and "broken-hearted" and "captive" and "blind" and "oppressed." That's one messy group! And that's the Church.

We're all together in one group, with all of our baggage and all of our wildly contrasting backgrounds. We have to work at unity, because disunity in the Church reveals a nasty spiritual disease. When that disunity involves incidentals—and yet continues over a prolonged period of time—we've got a deadly epidemic on our hands.

The Basics of Getting Along

So, what are the basics? What must we do and not do to get along with one another in the body of Christ? We see the basics clearly outlined in Philippians 2:3-4:

Let nothing be done through selfish ambition or

conceit, but in lowliness of mind let each

esteem others better than himself. Let each of

you look out not only for his own interests,

but also for the interests of others.

This very practical text gives us two ways of how *not* to be and to live and another two ways of how *to* be and to live.

How Not to Be and to Live

1. Don't Live Selfishly

Isaiah 14 describes Satan's attitude in Heaven before he fell. The devil said, *"I will ascend into heaven, I will exalt my throne above the stars of God; . . . I will be like the Most High"* (vv. 13-14).

Those verses describe selfish ambition and conceit—exactly what the passage in Philippians warns us against. Note that the first way we are *not* to act with each other is the very thing that got Satan kicked out of Heaven. We are never more like the devil than when we display the ungodly characteristic of proud selfishness.

Do you know a selfish person? Have you ever met a selfish individual? Well, do you have children or parents or a husband or a wife or friends? If so—if you know *any* human being—then you have encountered selfishness. Selfish ambition plagues *all* of humanity; it's one of our notable (but most regrettable) characteristics. It's been a natural human trait ever since the Fall.

Author Calvin Miller has said, "It's part of our nature to say, 'Our Father who art in Heaven, give me, give me, give me.'" That's just fallen human nature. The word translated "selfish ambition" in Philippians 2:3 means "to cause a division in a group so that you can get your own way"—that is, it refers to a manipulative, pushy person.

A little boy and his sister got a wooden rocking horse for Christmas. Their parents intended for them to share the present. One day they were both sitting on it, trying to ride the horse at the same time. Finally the little boy turned to his sister and said, "If one of us would get off, there'd be more room for me."

Selfish ambition is the "me first" philosophy that ruins marriages, friendships, and churches. Paul says, "Avoid it."

2. *Don't Live Pridefully*

Paul doesn't stop there, of course. He adds, "Let nothing be done through conceit." The King James Version uses a great phrase to translate the underlying Greek term: "vain [or empty] glory." The term *kenodoxia* means "the empty pride of living for people's favorable opinions." It refers to somebody who labors under an exaggerated opinion of himself or his own importance. Paul tells us in Romans 12:3 that we ought not to think of ourselves more highly than we ought to think, but rather, *"think soberly, as God has dealt to each one a measure of faith."*

It is no accident that Paul, Peter, and John all used the same word—"servant"—to introduce themselves in most of their New Testament letters. Paul liked to write, "Paul, a servant of the Lord Jesus Christ," or, "Paul, a servant of God and the Lord Jesus Christ." A more literal translation is "bondservant" or "bond-slave." *That's* how Paul saw himself. Rather than nurturing an exaggerated opinion of his own importance and living favorably for the opinions of others, Paul declared, "I'm a slave of the Lord Jesus Christ."

Do you consider yourself a servant—or a shopper? Are you a Christian—or a consumer? What do you see as your primary identity? What's it all about for you? If we want to get along in the church, the Bible insists we must get rid of our pride.

Somebody once said there are two ways to enter a room. You can say, "Hey, everybody, *here I am!*" (These words are usually communicated through actions more than words.)

Or you can say, "Ahh, *there* you are! What a treat to be with you!"

Paul says to us, "Don't live pridefully."

I thought of this the other day when I read an article about horse behavior. I learned that when a group of Thoroughbred horses is attacked, they defend themselves by forming a circle with their heads facing each other; then they all kick outward at the enemy. Donkeys have a very different approach. When a group of donkeys gets attacked, they all face outward and *kick each other*.

Which would you rather attend, a church of Thoroughbreds or a church of donkeys? The best way to avoid donkey behavior is to reject selfish and prideful living.

God instructs us to not kick each other, but to kick at the real enemy, Satan.

Okay, so much for the negatives. What are the basics of getting along in church from the positive side of the ledger?

How to Be and to Live

1. Live Humbly

Paul writes, *"In lowliness of mind let each esteem others better than himself"* (Philippians 2:3). To operate with "lowliness of mind" simply means to live with a humble spirit. When you live humbly, you immediately get on God's good side.

Did you know that living in pride instantly makes you God's enemy? The Bible says that God resists the proud, but gives grace to the humble (see James 4:6; 1 Peter 5:5). So if you want to stay on God's good side, consider yourself and project yourself as a humble servant of God, under His authority, and as just one member of His heavenly family.

When Paul wrote this instruction almost 2,000 years ago, "lowliness of mind" was considered a vice in the predominant Greek culture, not a virtue. The Greeks looked down on humble people. They considered humility something to be despised. The Greeks prided themselves on their "superior" culture—anything not Greek, they considered "barbarian." Whenever they conquered an outside group, they called the vanquished people "humble-minded." They'd say, "We conquered them; they're lowly-minded, humble. Despicable!"

The Greeks believed in self-assertiveness, self-confidence, and self-esteem, not in lowliness of mind. They would have loved Clint Eastwood's Harry Callahan: "Go ahead, make my day." They would have loved the Terminator: "I'll be back."

Paul, on the other hand, took this idea so despised by the Greeks and elevated it from a vice to a virtue. "If you want to get along with others," he said, "be lowly in mind." And why did he do this? We find the answer in Philippians 2:5-8:

> *Let this mind be in you which was also in Christ Jesus, who, being in the form of God, did not consider it robbery to be equal with God, but made Himself of no reputation, taking the form of a bondservant, and coming in the likeness of men. And being found in appearance as a man, He humbled Himself and became obedient to the point of death, even the death of the cross.*

Paul elevated humility as a virtue because Jesus practiced it. Christ humbled himself, even though He was the very Son of God. When He left the glories of Heaven to become a man, Jesus humbled himself more than we'll ever know. So we can trust Him when He says, "*Take My yoke upon you and learn from Me, for I am gentle and lowly in heart*"

(Matthew 11:29). Jesus Christ is our chief example.

If you want to get along with others, Paul insists, don't be selfish or prideful; be humble-minded instead. "Don't take your cues from the world," Paul counsels us, "but from Jesus, who was lowly and humble in mind."

In fact, lowliness of mind—humility—is the grease that keeps the wheels of the church running smoothly. A humble spirit keeps us flowing along together in harmony and peace. Jesus would tell us, "Don't climb higher to get more noticed but be willing to climb lower to serve more effectively."

One of my favorite authors is F.B. Meyer, an English pastor and evangelist who died in 1929. Meyer wrote very clearly about this issue. "I used to think that God's gifts were on shelves one above the other, and that the taller we grew in Christian character the more easily we could reach them," he wrote. "I now find that God's gifts are on shelves one beneath the other, and that it's not a question of growing taller but of stooping lower."[2]

Do you want a rewarding church experience? Then get down. I don't mean, "Get down with your bad self!" I mean get humble, become lowly. And how can you cultivate humility? You can't simply say, "Today I'm going to be humble." Humility has to be nurtured. So let me suggest a few ways to grow it.

- *Prayer*

Prayer naturally cultivates humility. When you pray, you declare that you don't have the resources to depend on yourself. You are saying, "I depend on God." No prideful person prays much because he doesn't think he needs God much. If you want to cultivate humility, then get serious about prayer.

---

2. See Endnotes, page 248.

- *Genuine worship*

When we gather as a church to worship, we cultivate humility. We consciously focus on the grandeur and majesty of God. We celebrate His love that rescued us from our sin, and we praise Him for His grace that keeps us breathing. Genuine worship reminds us how great God is and how small we are—and yet it brings us directly into His glorious presence as His dearly loved children.

- *Do something not required*

Take on a task that no one assigned to you. By doing so you say, "I'm going to be a bondservant. I'm going to pick up that paper. I'm going to clean that toilet. I'm going to help out these under-resourced folks or befriend this lonely person." By reaching down, you actually reach up.

- *Encourage, affirm, and thank people*

None of us would be where we are today without the help of others. There are no "self-made" men or women. When you genuinely and enthusiastically encourage, affirm, and thank the people in your life, you grow in humility and the church grows in grace. Do you want to grow tall spiritually? Then learn to bow gratefully before God and before others.

2. *Live Respectfully*

Once you humble yourself, it becomes far easier to treat people with the respect they deserve as men and women created in God's image. And yet, our culture doesn't encourage us to respect others, does it? It encourages us to admire ourselves, first and foremost.

It has become standard fare in our society to exalt the "virtue" of self-esteem. It's everywhere. It appeared several years ago on *Saturday Night Live* when a silly character named Stuart Smalley continually said to himself, "I'm good enough, I'm nice enough, and doggone it, people like me."

He repeated this personal mantra to himself, as he gazed lovingly in the mirror, to develop his own self-esteem.

Yet Paul tells us, "Let each esteem others better than himself." The Williams translation renders Paul's words, "Practice treating one another as a superior."[3] And how can we do this, especially when it's so contrary to our culture? Verse 4 answers, "*Let each of you look out* [the Greek word means "focus carefully; watch and observe others"] *not only for his own interests, but also for the interests of others.*"

If I always put myself first and you always put yourself first, then sooner rather than later we're going to collide. But if I'm consciously looking out for you and your best interests and you're consciously looking out for me and my best interests, then we're going to build a strong, healthy, and happy church.

A boy was talking to his friend one day when off the cuff he said, "Wouldn't you just hate to wear glasses all the time?"

His little buddy shook his head and replied, "I don't know—I don't think I'd mind it so much if they were like my grandma's glasses."

"What do you mean?" asked the first boy, perplexed.

"Well," his friend answered, "my grandma has the ability to see when someone is hurting or in pain or in need, and she knows exactly what to do to help them. So I asked her once, 'Grandma, how can you see that way all the time?' She said, 'It must be my age. Ever since I've gotten older, it's just the way I see life and people.'"

The first boy scratched his head and said, "You're right. It must be her glasses."

---

3. See Endnotes, page 248.

May God give us all such glasses! May God give us a vision transplant so we can see and focus on others' hurts, pains, and anxieties. That is the best and most effective way to live respectfully with one another and so manage to get along in church.

The Basis of Getting Along

Now that we've considered the basics of getting along, what's the basis for it? What is its purpose? Why should we get along? We find the answers in Philippians 2:1-2:

> *Therefore if there is any consolation in Christ, if any comfort of love, if any fellowship of the Spirit, if any affection and mercy, fulfill my joy by being like-minded, having the same love, being of one accord, of one mind.*

This text suggests four key reasons why we should work hard to get along with each other in the Church, Jesus' Body.

Reason One: You Need the Support

Why should you learn to get along with others in church? Answer: *The world won't provide any support for you.*

The world will never supply a loving, caring, nurturing environment for you as a believer in Christ. In fact, you live in a world sharply hostile to Christians—so you had better work to create a loving environment in the church.

The first word in Philippians 2 is "Therefore," which immediately calls our attention to something the apostle wrote earlier. He didn't originally write his letters in chapters; verse references got added hundreds of years later so we could more easily refer to various parts of the Bible. When Paul wrote, he wrote a seamless, complete letter. So when the apostle writes, "therefore," we should look at what it's there for.

It turns out that it's there for a very important reason. Paul ties his thoughts in chapter 2 to what he wrote just before in ask:

> *Only let your conduct be worthy of the gospel of Christ, so that whether I come and see you or am absent, I may hear of your affairs, that you stand fast in one spirit, with one mind striving together for the faith of the gospel, and not in any way terrified by your adversaries, which is to them a proof of perdition, but to you of salvation, and that from God. For to you it has been granted on behalf of Christ, not only to believe in Him, but also to suffer for His sake, having the same conflict which you saw in me and now hear is in me. Therefore . . .* (Philippians 1:27-30)

Paul is saying, "Look, the world won't provide you with the kind of love and support and encouragement that you need to thrive in your relationship with God. It has no interest in supplying you with a nurturing environment since it hates everything you stand for. So the only place you'll get what you need to grow in grace—the only place to expect it—is among fellow believers. As you gather in church, remember that you are called-out saints in need of true fellowship."

Jesus declared much the same thing when He said, "*In the world you will have tribulation; but be of good cheer, I have overcome the world*" (John 16:33). And how did He "overcome the world"? One big way Jesus overcame the world was by providing for us a loving family, which He called "the Church."

Can you name the most popular daily TV genre? What's number one? Answer: soap operas. And what are the basic themes of soap operas? Answer: disunity, hatred, avarice, deceit, envy, jealousy. (Of course, the many characters having affairs usually get along with each other pretty well—until they break up. Then the fur *really* flies!) The most popular shows on daily television feature a flock of beautiful people acting in the ugliest of ways.

This is why it looks so awkward for Christians to be fighting each other in church; it far too closely resembles the world. An unbeliever goes to the average church and says, "Hey, I can get *this* on a soap opera. I don't need to come to church for *this*."

There are few things more tragic than churches riddled with bitterness, hateful words, harsh accusations, and even lawsuits. Listen—we had better create an environment of love and acceptance in the church, because we surely won't find it anywhere else.

Reason Two: You Belong to Jesus

Paul then gives another reason why you should strive to make the church a loving, supportive fellowship: *You belong to Christ.*

"Therefore," Paul writes, "If [or "since"] there is any consolation in Christ..." What does it mean to be "in Christ?" It means He accepts us. It means He forgives us. So on that basis—that Christ loves us and accepts us and forgives us—we should work hard to get along with others "in Christ" and love them and accept them and forgive them.

Remember what Jesus taught us to pray? *"Our Father who art in heaven, Hallowed be Your name. Your kingdom come, Your will be done on earth as it is in heaven. Give us this day our daily bread and forgive us our debts as we forgive our debtors"* (Matthew 6:9-12). On that basis—that

I am consoled by being "in Christ"—Jesus instructs me to forgive and accept others.

Elsewhere Paul wrote, *"Be kind to one another, tenderhearted, forgiving one another, even as God in Christ forgave you"* (Ephesians 4:32). People can be nasty, brutish, thick-headed, and inconsiderate, can't they? They say mean and stupid things, don't they? That's precisely why they need to be forgiven. And who better to forgive them than those of us who know and serve Jesus Christ?

A gravestone in a cemetery just outside of New York has a single word carved on it. It offers no name, no date of birth, no date of death, no epitaph—just one word: "Forgiven." Can you think of a better word to put on a gravestone? Well, maybe there's one: "Forgiving." The words go hand-in-hand. Since I'm forgiven, I can be forgiving.

Reason Three: Jesus Loves You

Why should you work at making your church a place of love and forgiveness? Answer: *Jesus loves you.*

"If there is any consolation in Christ," Paul writes, "if any comfort of love. . . " Do you know whose love Paul has in mind? The love of Christ. Jesus' love for us is the catalyst for our own love. And God's love is the greatest provision for our comfort.

As a kid, did you like the fairy tale about the beautiful princess who had to kiss the ugly toad in order to turn him back into a handsome prince? Most kids love that story—but have you ever thought about it from the princess's viewpoint? Would you want to plant *your* lips on a grimy, greasy, green toad? What princess in her right mind would stoop down and say, "Oh, what a joy to kiss such a loathsome amphibian!" Don't get me wrong, it's *great* for the toad—"Here comes my love, my beautiful, kissing princess!"—but for the princess's sake, we can be relieved that it's only a fairy tale.

Yet God, through Christ, in love stooped down to kiss us toads! Please don't take offense at that. For that's just what He did: *"But God demonstrates His own love toward us, in that while we were still sinners, Christ died for us"* (Romans 5:8). God gave us *everything*. His love was the catalyst for His salvation.

And then He went even further when He put His love *into* us: *"The love of God has been poured out in our hearts by the Holy Spirit who was given to us,"* Paul writes (Romans 5:5). Because of this, you and I now have an enormous capacity to love. We don't always express it, of course, nor do we always feel it. But as Christians, we have an enormous capacity to love, and God has given us this capacity. Because we have received His love, the apostle says, we should also distribute His love.

Reason Four: You're Part of His Family

Why should you work hard to get along with others in church? Here's a fourth reason: *You are part of a spiritual family.*

Paul writes, "If there is any consolation in Christ, if any comfort of love, if any fellowship of the Spirit, if any affection and mercy..." God has made us to be part of a heavenly partnership, a spiritual family.

The Greek term *koinonia* (here translated "fellowship") means "a joint partnership in something of common interest." In other words, in the church we share spiritual blessings and spiritual resources. As a spiritual family, we express what Paul calls "affection and mercy." That means that as members of the family of God, our compassion toward one another ought to be high, while our finger-pointing should be low.

Paul further writes, "Fulfill my joy"—in other words, "Make me really happy as an apostle." And how could the Philippians make Paul smile? The apostle answers, "By being like-minded, having the same love, being of one accord, of one mind."

We are not merely individuals of faith who gather periodically to sharpen our separate spiritual resumes. We are instead a family of God, a body of Christ, a group of believers in Christ who need their brothers and sisters in the Lord to become the community God intends us to be.

A Lot Is at Stake

Can't we all just get along? Yes, we can—*if* we learn to value one another and love one another as God loves us.

I heard a story about a young soldier who was returning home from war. As soon as he arrived in his own country, he called his mother long-distance. Each felt great excitement at hearing the other's voice; it had been a *long* time. After catching up for a while, the young man said, "Mom, I have my best friend in the whole world here with me. I want to bring him home. He saved my life. He was one of my buddies in the field, and when a hand grenade got thrown into our foxhole, he got seriously wounded saving my life."

He paused, then continued tentatively, "As a result, he has only one eye, one arm, and one leg. He doesn't have any family except ours, Mom." With hope rising in his voice, he said, "I told him that he could come home with me. I would like your permission for him to come and be part of our family and live with us from now on. Can he?" He then stopped, waiting anxiously for the reply.

"You bring him home, son," his mother said, "and in a few days we'll be able to find a place for him where I know he'll be happy. I'm so anxious to see you!" She tried hard to hold back the tears she felt welling up in her eyes.

"Mother," the young soldier pleaded, "I want him to come and be a part of *our* family. Not to go anywhere else, but to live with us."

The mother sighed and said, "Son, you're so young. I'm sure it would be all right for a short time, but after a while he'd get tired of always having to be here, and we'd get tired of always having to care for him. You can bring him home for three or four weeks, and during that time we'll find a good place for him. You understand, don't you?"

The young man's voice trailed off as he said, "Yes, mother. I think I do."

They said their goodbyes and hung up. The young soldier's mother could hardly wait to see her son in a few days. She had waited so long! But the next day, a government official stopped by the home with tragic news. The young soldier had taken his own life. Shocked and perplexed, the grieving mother wondered how such a horrible thing could have happened.

A few days later, her son's body arrived in his hometown. Numb with grief, the weeping mother went down to view the body of her precious son. She looked into the coffin—and immediately understood. He had only one eye, one arm, and one leg. He had tested her love on the phone—and it had fallen short. He felt sure that as a person with severe handicaps, he no longer had any value . . . and so he had taken his life.

We are compelled to love others without conditions because Jesus accepts us unconditionally. Can't we all just get along? Surely we can. We must! The love of Jesus compels us.

CHAPTER 6

How to Build
A Beautiful Body

King David once took a look at his body and said to the Lord, "*I am fearfully and wonderfully made*" (Psalm 139:14). The New Living Translation put the king's sentiment a little bit differently. It says, "Thank you for making me so wonderfully complex!"

And we are! Our bodies are divine engineering marvels.

God has created your body with about thirty *trillion* cells, give or take a few million. Inside each cell lies a nucleus and inside each nucleus hums a world of activity, including twenty-three pairs of chromosomes—one set that you got from your mom and one that you got from your dad. Those chromosomes contain DNA, scrunched up like a tape. Densely coded and compacted DNA information dictates how every cell of your body will operate from birth until death. They determine the color of your hair (so long as you have some), what body type you will have, how tall you will grow, and everything else about your physical makeup.

If you were to take the genetic information inside the nucleus of a single cell from your body and translate it into written information, such as a book, you could fill a library with 4,000 volumes.[1] That's an astounding amount of information in just one cell! So how big of a storage room do you suppose you would need if you were to translate all thirty trillion cells of your body and put it into books?

The information would fill up the Grand Canyon—*seventy-five times over!*[2] Since the Grand Canyon is between three to twenty miles wide and 200 miles long, it's something of an understatement to say, "We are fearfully and wonderfully made."

The Bible also speaks about another body: the Body of Christ. In fact, it's one of the Apostle Paul's favorite metaphors to describe the Church of Jesus Christ—and it's just as amazing as its counterpart! Paul deftly uses the image when he writes to the church at Corinth, which was, unfortunately, a fractured, broken body. This group of believers hardly qualified for the word beautiful.

Paul desperately wanted it to reflect the beauty of Christ, however, so in 1 Corinthians 12 he went to great depth to show his friends how to bring health and vitality back into their struggling fellowship. Here I'd like to dip into Paul's God-given wisdom to offer four "bodybuilding" tips that will help us to build a strong church body.

Tip One: Recognize the Variety

How can we build a strong local fellowship of believers? Paul counsels us to *recognize the great variety in Christ's body, the Church*. God did not create us as individuals so that we could all look and act exactly like each other. In fact, He wants us to celebrate our differences:

---

1. See Endnotes, page 248.
2. See Endnotes, page 248.

> *There are diversities* [a wide variety] *of gifts, but the same Spirit. There are differences of ministries, but the same Lord. And there are diversities of activities, but it is the same God who works all in all. But the manifestation of the Spirit is given to each one for the profit of all: for to one is given the word of wisdom through the Spirit, to another the word of knowledge through the same Spirit, to another faith by the same Spirit, to another gifts of healings by the same Spirit, to another the working of miracles, to another prophecy, to another discerning of spirits, to another different kinds of tongues, to another the interpretation of tongues. But one and the same Spirit works all these things, distributing to each one individually as He wills.* 1 Corinthians 12:4-11

God does not choose to work solely through one gift or ministry or style or group or denomination. On the contrary, our God is a God of variety. He *loves* variety, in fact—so we ought to love it as well.

Imagine what it would be like if at Christmas everyone gave you exactly the same present. Wouldn't that get pretty boring?

Or what if every day of your year looked exactly the same as the previous day? Have you ever seen the movie *Groundhog Day*? Comedian Bill Murray finds himself waking up to the identical set of circumstances, day after day: The alarm clock goes off at precisely the same time, the same song plays, and Murray's character has to figure out why he's stuck in an endless loop—and then do something different to break it.

What if every place on Earth looked identical to every other place on Earth? Where would you go on vacation?

As God has put variety in His creation, so He has put variety in the Body of Christ. The church—every church—has a variety of people with different backgrounds and dissimilar gifts. This is all a part of God's good design.

That means we should never try to force everyone into the same spiritual mold. I worry sometimes that this is exactly what we do. We want to get them saved and then stick them in a one-size-fits-all mold: "You are to think this way, like these songs, read from this version of the Bible—and then I'll feel better about you."

Such a strategy never pleases God, however; for just as there is variety in the mind and heart of God, so He wants variety in the Body of Christ.

Somebody once sent me the following joke:

> *There are 200 million Americans; 86 million are over sixty-five and 76 million are under twenty-one. That leaves only 38 million to do the work—but 6 million are in the armed forces, so that leaves 32 million to do the work. Another 6 million are on welfare, so that only leaves 26 million to do the work. Fifteen million work for the government, so that leaves 11 million to do the work. Ten million are in school, so that leaves 1 million to do the work. But 750,000 are disabled or sick, so that leaves 250,000 left to do the work. Last week there were 249,998 people in jail, so that leaves only two people to do the work—and since you don't do very much, no wonder I'm so tired!*

You want to know the truth? If the variety of gifts and people that God created would get involved as God intended, *no one* would feel tired.

"*There are differences of ministries,*" Paul writes, "*but the same Lord. And there are diversities of activities, but it is the same God who works all in all*" (vv. 5-6). Take two or five or fifty people with the same spiritual gift, and you'll see it expressed differently in each one. Why? Because there are different manifestations of the same gift. That's beautiful variety!

If you were to give Chuck Swindoll and Raul Ries the identical passage of Scripture and have them each preach a sermon on it, I guarantee that what comes out would be different! Each man manifests the same gift differently—exactly as God intended.

The same is true with evangelism. One might have the gift of an evangelist, like Billy Graham, and be able to stand in front of thousands to preach the gospel, feeling very much at home. Yet if you give another person, equally gifted, the opportunity to stand in front of a similar crowd, he will shake and quiver, and his tongue will stick to the roof of his mouth. Why? Because he doesn't *like* being in front of a crowd—even though he too has the gift of an evangelist. He might prefer to knock on doors, speak to total strangers face-to-face, and cold turkey—without a prior relationship—share the gospel. Not everybody can do that! I know some people who would knock on the door and then silently pray, "Dear Jesus, may nobody be home!" They are afraid of "cold turkey" evangelism. But in a casual setting, such as over a cup of coffee or by writing a very personal letter, they might very powerfully share the gospel. These Christians have the same gift yet different expressions.

We can never confine God to a box, to a single method, to a certain style, to a particular group, to a solitary organization, or to one denomination alone. If you want a dramatic demonstration of His variety, then just observe how Jesus healed various people. Did Jesus heal in the same way every time? No. Sometimes He did nothing but speak a word; at other times He would lay His hands on the sick; on one occasion He touched the person twice before the healing took place; on another occasion He grabbed some dirt, spat on it, made a mud ball, and wiped it on the man's eyes. Jesus used different methods and different styles at different times.

And who controls all of this variety of gifts? Paul answers, *"But one and the same Spirit works all these things, distributing to each one individually as He wills"*

(v. 11). This tells me that the church is all about what *He* wills and what *He* wants. Therefore, I can't say, "It's my church," and you can't say it's your church. It's *His* church, and thus church isn't about getting my will or your will done, but about us participating in getting *His* will accomplished. *He* is the One who controls the variety.

Tip Two: Emphasize Unity

The second bodybuilding tip advises us to emphasize unity. Paul writes:

> *For as the body is one and has many members, but all the members of that one body, being many, are one body, so also is Christ. For by one Spirit we were all baptized into one body—whether Jews or Greeks, whether slaves or free—and have all been made to drink into one Spirit. For in fact the body is not one member but many.* 1 Corinthians 12:12-14

Although we are to *recognize* the beautifully diverse variety in the church, we are to *emphasize* unity. Here's why: If we focus on the first part and not the second part, the body will soon get totally out of whack. It's going to malfunction. If I'm celebrating and emphasizing variety—but I don't say that we all have to be going in the same direction—then every member could quickly start doing his or her own thing, thus creating division rather than unity.

Who does the Bible name as the head of the Body of Christ? *Jesus.* In your own body, your brain tells the rest of the body what to do and when to do it. If everything is working well and functioning as it should, then your body enjoys a smooth, unified set of activities. In the Body of Christ, Jesus is the brain. He is the one telling the hand, the leg, the foot, and all the other parts of the body what to do and when to do it. He's the one giving the orders.

The Holy Spirit works as something like the body's nervous system. He takes our directions from the brain, Jesus, and then transmits them to all parts of the body. Thus He enables all parts to fulfill their intended functions—making possible the smooth functioning of the body.

When your body operates as intended, it presents a wonderful example of teamwork. A message goes to the brain from the stomach, "I'm hungry. I'm empty. Please fill me up." So the brain sends a message to the legs, "Walk to the barbeque." The nose smells the onions; the eyes spot the burger; the hands grab it—and soon it's in the mouth and gone. Every part of the body works together for the smooth functioning of the whole.

But what if the leg should say, "No way! I'm not going"? Thankfully, it usually doesn't because the brain controls the whole process, getting all the members to cooperate. If one or more of those members decides not to cooperate, however, then you have a big problem. We usually call it a disease. And a diseased body is no fun at all.

I thank God that I've nearly always had a healthy body. One evening years ago, however, I started to feel sick to my stomach while driving home after a Bible study. I had eaten a burrito and wondered if I might be suffering from food poisoning. So I asked my buddy, who had also eaten a burrito, "Was there something bad in the food we ate? Because I'm not feeling very well."

"No," he said, "I feel great."

I felt more and more sick over the two-hour drive. I went to bed as soon as I got home, but I woke up at 2 a.m., doubled over in pain. I couldn't move. *Something* was clearly wrong, but what? I had no idea.

Since my wife was out of town, I called my friend, who took me to the hospital. After running several tests, the doctor told me, "We've determined that something is wrong with you, but we don't know what it is." They kept me in the hospital for a few more days, ran more tests—and still couldn't figure out the problem.

Finally, a young surgeon walked into my room and said, "Since none of the tests we have run tell us anything specific, I'm going to do exploratory surgery. If your white blood cell count doesn't go down by tomorrow morning"—I had some kind of unknown infection—"I'm going to cut you open."

"Oh, really?" I replied.

"Oh, yes," she answered. *"Really."* She wanted to do one more test to see if they could determine what I had.

"What kind of test?" I asked.

"A barium enema," she answered.

Since I have a medical background, I knew *exactly* what was coming. I had always been on the giving end of them; now I was to be on the receiving end.

Lying on the X-ray table right before the exam, I thought about what Job had said: *"For the thing I greatly feared has come upon me"* (Job 3:25). My fear came upon me at that moment—and all because one member of my body was not cooperating. And to this day, I still don't know which one it was.

By the next morning, my white blood cell count had gone down, I didn't have to have exploratory surgery, and the doctors released me from the hospital. The young surgeon said she wanted to see me in a week. I didn't show up—hey, I'm not going back to see *anyone* so eager to cut me open!

During my period of illness, I thought about the parts of my body. *Which one of you isn't cooperating with the rest of the body?* I wondered. I had plenty of individuality and variety, but not nearly enough unity.

Growing up, I had a friend who suffered from multiple sclerosis. In him, I saw how a horrible disease could ravage the human body. In the first years of our friendship, I knew him as healthy, strong, and vibrant; but as his disease progressed, he began losing motor control and his bodily motions began to look increasingly jerky and uncoordinated. Why? Doctors tell us that in victims of multiple sclerosis, the cerebral cortex and the spinal cord develop hardened patches so that the brain's messages don't transmit smoothly. Instead of the brain's messages moving unhindered to each part of the body, the messages get interrupted—and paralysis eventually sets in.

It makes me wonder what the world sees when it observes the Church. Too often, I fear, instead of saying, "WOW! What a wonderful, beautiful group! It operates so smoothly!" they see a spastic, paralyzed kind of body. This observation fails to be attractive for many of them.

One of Satan's biggest traps—and it is a trap—is to get us fighting one another so that we have no energy left to fight him, the real enemy. In that case, he's free to continue his work of sending people to hell. How crucial it is that we recognize variety in church even as we emphasize its unity!

Tip Three: Maximize Equality

One of the reasons church groups malfunction is that certain gifted individuals—let's just call them "gifts in the body"—get placed on a higher pedestal than the rest of us. "Oooh, now that gift is more important than those gifts," people say. But whenever that happens, a malfunction occurs. Paul writes:

> *If the foot should say, "Because I am not a hand, I am not of the body," is it therefore not of the body? And if the ear should say, "Because I am not an eye, I am not of the body," is it therefore not of the body? If the whole body were an eye, where would be the hearing? If the whole were hearing, where would be the smelling? But now God has set the members, each one of them, in the body just as He pleased. And if they were all one member, where would the body be? But now indeed there are many members, yet one body.* 1 Corinthians 12:15-20

If you have unity without variety, then you have uniformity—and that's boring. If you have variety without unity, you have anarchy—everybody does his own thing, resulting in chaos. The solution is found in the third element that Paul spotlights for us: equality. *All* of the members of the body, though quite different from each other, are equally important.

How does Paul emphasize this point? He identifies a few parts of the body that are most visible—the ones we usually see first—and compares them with other parts of the body that get much less attention. It's hard not to see a person's hands, for example (especially if they're Italian; they tend to move a lot). We shake hands, not feet (which we usually cover). We work with our hands; we wave them. Have you ever seen a person wave his foot out the window to greet you? It just doesn't happen.

And yet we absolutely need our feet and legs. How else would we get around? We might see the hand more often than we see the foot, but both are equally important for the proper functioning of the body.

The same is true with our eyes and ears. What do most of us notice when we first meet someone? For me, it's the eyes. I immediately notice eye color. The first time I met Lenya, it was her eyes that grabbed me. I noticed her lovely eyebrows, the roundness of her eyes and their amazing color. I thought, *Beautiful eyes!* I don't remember being charmed by her ears or even noticing them. I didn't walk away from our encounter thinking, *Wow, what great lobes!*

Truth be told, ears are ugly—but we need them. God fashioned them as they are to efficiently direct sound from our environment into the inner ear, so that we can understand and perceive our environment. Both eyes and ears are necessary. Paul asks, "If the whole body were an eye, where would be the hearing?"

When you read the Bible, do you ever stop to let the author's words really soak in? When I read this verse, I picture a five-foot-seven eyeball—and I think, *That has to be the ugliest thing I've ever seen*. What good is a five-foot-seven eyeball? Do you put it in the back of your car and drive it around so it can see the neighborhood? It doesn't have a mouth, so it can't even tell you what it sees. It doesn't have an ear, so it can't perceive the sounds in its environment. Really, what good is it?

And that's the apostle's point: It's useless to emphasize one part of the body over all the other parts. Yet this is exactly what we do whenever we put certain gifts on pedestals and say, "*That* is an important gift, far more so than *those*. *That* person is much more valuable than *those* people." We make at least two serious errors when we engage in the pedestal mentality.

Number One: We set up people for failure. Anytime you place someone on a pedestal, you prepare him for a fall. And the further you push him up, the greater the distance he has to plummet.

Number Two: You send the following message to the rest of the church: "You're really not very important." In fact, many will walk away thinking, *I'm definitely not a hand or an eye, so I must not be part of the body at all.*

Back in March of 1981, John Hinckley, Jr. shot Ronald Reagan, the president of the United States of America, and Reagan had to spend a couple of weeks in the hospital recovering from his wounds. So did the United States shut down during that time? Of course not. It went on almost as normal because the Constitution lays out a clear chain of command in the event that anything should happen to the president.

But what would happen if all the garbage collectors in America suddenly stopped working? Several years ago in Philadelphia, their strike nearly shut down the city. Experts have studied what happened, and they tell us that if all of the nation's garbage collectors were to go on strike, the United States of America would come to a screeching halt *within three weeks.*

So then—who is more important, the president or the nation's garbage collectors? *Everyone* is important. The president is certainly an important person with a vital job to do. But garbage collectors are also very important, and they too have important jobs.

Just because a job is unnoticed, doesn't mean it is unimportant.

You can lose a hand, an eye, or a foot and still live, however you can't lose your heart or your pituitary gland and expect the same result.

Do you ever think about your pituitary gland? You can't see it, so it usually goes unnoticed.

Have you ever gone up to a friend and asked, "I've just been wondering lately—how's your pituitary gland?" I doubt it. You just don't think about things like pituitary glands unless something goes wrong with them. We don't notice them until they cause a problem. This example confirms my statement that just because it is unnoticed, does not mean it is unimportant.

In fact, I would say that most parts of a healthy body—and equally, a healthy church—are unseen. They go largely unnoticed. It's those prayer warriors and those selfless, faithful servants behind the scenes who keep everything running so smoothly. That is why, in the church, there is an equality of importance.

Tip Four: Minimize Self-sufficiency

We American Christians need this fourth lesson perhaps most of all because we live in a culture that worships self-sufficiency. It's bred into us. But notice what Paul says:

> *And the eye cannot say to the hand, "I have no need of you"; nor again the head to the feet, "I have no need of you." No, much rather, those members of the body which seem to be weaker are necessary.* 1 Corinthians 12:21-22

More than once I've met a person who has told me, "Yes, I am a Christian. I love Jesus Christ—but I don't go to church regularly, because, you see, I don't believe in organized religion. I don't need the church to grow as a Christian."

That, my friends, is a lie. God did not build us to be independent. He fashioned us to become interdependent. If we want to thrive as believers in Christ, we can never say, "I don't need you." The truth is that we need each other, and deeply. God calls us to get integrated into each other's lives.

Listen, you never even would have *heard* the gospel unless somebody had explained it to you. "Oh, no," you say, "that's not true. I heard it on the radio" or, "I watched a television program." Fine—but some *person* broadcast that message in words you could understand, while other people behind the scenes put the program together so you could hear it. None of us would ever grow in Christ unless some other person helped us to grow in Christ. I'm no exception and neither are you.

How It Fits Together

The Book of Acts describes a crisis that upset the early church. A nasty split had occurred between two groups of ladies in the Jerusalem congregation, some of whom had a Greek heritage and some of whom spoke Hebrew. When the church told the apostles about this division, note what happened:

> *Then the twelve summoned the multitude of the disciples and said, "It is not desirable that we should leave the word of God and serve tables. Therefore, brethren, seek out from among you seven men of good reputation, full of the Holy Spirit and wisdom, whom we may appoint over this business; but we will give ourselves continually to prayer and to the ministry of the word."*
>
> *And the saying pleased the whole multitude. And they chose Stephen, a man full of faith and the Holy Spirit, and Philip, Prochorus, Nicanor, Timon, Parmenas, and Nicolas, a proselyte from Antioch, whom they set before the apostles; and when they*

> *had prayed, they laid hands on them. Then the word of God spread, and the number of the disciples multiplied greatly in Jerusalem, and a great many of the priests were obedient to the faith.* Acts 6:2-7

In this passage, spiritual people met a spiritual problem with spiritual priorities. So what did they do?

Number One: They recognized variety. They said, "Not all of us are apostles. Some people among us have the gift of service. Let's find them."

Number Two: They emphasized unity. "We're not going to leave the Word of God to serve tables," the apostles said. "Find seven capable men from among you—not from the outside, but from within."

Number Three: They maximized equality. While the church at large chose the seven men who would oversee the new ministry, the apostles got behind them and said, "Yes, we agree with you. We're on the same page and we're all at the same level." And so the church continued to move forward.

Number Four: They minimized self-sufficiency. Everybody in the church said, "Okay, great! If that's the plan, then we'll go with it. We'll listen to the apostles and we'll follow the seven men the church has chosen to lead this effort. It's a good plan." Not one of them said, "Hey, I didn't get my way, so I'm leaving."

You see, it works. And it will work just as well today.

Listen to the Monkeys

Dr. Harry F. Harlow, a researcher at the University of Wisconsin, wanted to understand what kind of contact human babies need with adult humans. By observing the behavior of baby monkeys and investigating their social practices, he hoped to extrapolate some important lessons for humans.

He put eight baby monkeys in cages and over time changed several variables in their environment. Quickly, he noticed the baby monkeys seemed emotionally attached to cloth pads lying at the bottom of their cages. These baby monkeys would caress the cloth pads, cuddle them, and treat them just like a child would treat a teddy bear.

Eventually, Harlow made a surrogate mother out of some terrycloth—a little bit of soft fabric that somehow looked like a mother monkey. He put a light bulb behind it, placed a rubber nipple in front of it, and made a feeding tube protrude from it. Next he constructed a second surrogate mother, only this one was made completely out of wire mesh—but again with the rubber nipple and feeding tube.

The eight baby monkeys spent almost all of their waking hours around the terrycloth mother: cuddling her, caressing her, getting warm by her, playing on her, perched on her.

Harlow then took four of the eight monkeys and trained them to eat from the wire mesh mother. The other four continued to eat from the terrycloth surrogate. The monkeys trained to eat from the wire mesh mother did eat from her—but they continued to cuddle the terrycloth mother.

Then the doctor isolated some of the monkeys into cages made of nothing but wire mesh: wire mesh floors, wire mesh mothers, and no terrycloth at all. These monkeys did feed from the new surrogate mother—but then they cowered in the corner, screaming. Many did not survive.

Harlow's conclusion? We humans need more than food if we are to survive. We need warm touch and soft, cuddly interaction.[3]

Let's not become wire mesh Christians! Let's not make church just a place where we go to wolf down a spiritual meal. If we come merely to listen to a sermon and to get a little spiritual food, then let's not call it church because it's really not a body. It's only a mouth.

A body needs all of its parts functioning and working together. A body is never about one part but about *all* of its parts growing, learning, giving, and receiving together. So take a cue from the monkeys. Get involved personally and deeply in the life of your church. As you get more involved in the local church, you will find yourself in the corner, screaming a whole lot less.

---

3. See Endnotes, page 248.

CHAPTER 7

Church-Building

101

What would you consider to be the most exciting room in a hospital? I figure it's probably the delivery room. You find a lot of joy in those places! The delivery room is great fun, but it's also confusing and noisy and a buzzing beehive of continual activity.

I suspect that the birth of the Church had a lot in common with a hospital delivery room. Most maternity wards consider themselves busy if they deliver twenty babies on the same day—and yet, at Pentecost, *3,000* brand-new babes in Christ joined His Body! You can bet it was an exciting and fun time, but it was also a time full of noise and confusion and non-stop, bewildering activity.

Nothing but Jesus

As I was growing up, every now and then my dad would say something like, "Skip, *how* many times do I have to tell you this before you'll finally get the message?"

"A lot of times, Dad." Too often, I just didn't "get" the message.

Did you know in the Bible, God has told us about His Church *one hundred eighteen* times? How important do you figure church must be to God if He speaks of it so often in His eternal Word?

Before He went to the Cross, Jesus declared, *"I will build My church"* (Matthew 16:18), and in Acts 2 we see the Lord beginning to do just that. Since this is one of the most important passages in the entire Bible on who we are and what we do as the Church—we could call it a passage of primary reference—we need to look at it very carefully.

Remember that the first church didn't have buildings, public address systems, policy manuals, or seasoned leaders. In fact, we would have found the church a very fluid, unruly, and disorganized thing—and it was all God's fault. After all, *He* added those 3,000 souls to the Church that day!

If you had asked Peter a few weighty theological questions as God brought the Church into existence, I doubt he would have been able to articulate his answers in a satisfying way, even though he knew his Bible very well. If you had said to him, "Peter, tell me about your eschatology. Are you premillennial, amillennial, or postmillenial? And when you're through with that, please tell me a little something about your ecclesiology." I believe he would have looked at you and said, "*Huh*?" And then he might have added, "All I know is that I'm doing what Jesus told me to do. I love Him and I'm following Him. He said He would build His Church, and I'm just glad to be a part of it."

That's about all the Church had at this stage in history. It wasn't much more than, "Jesus is doing something wonderful here, and we are glad to be a part of it."

Back in the early '70s, an article in the newspaper quoted some local Christian leader who had his own opinion of the earnest young kids then flocking to Christ through the

Jesus Movement. "Well," he said disdainfully, "all they have is Jesus."

And that's a bad thing? What else do you need?

I'm not saying that theology is unimportant or that organization is irrelevant. But I am saying that when *anything* eclipses the centrality of Jesus Christ, something has gone deeply wrong.

Let Him In!

The Book of Revelation contains seven letters written to seven churches in Asia Minor, dictated by the resurrected Jesus himself. To one church He said, "You're doing a lot of great things. You're very busy and very active— but I do have something against you. You have left your first love . . . Me" (see Revelation 2:2-4).

Did you hear of the woman who five times tried unsuccessfully to join a church? The church was an upscale, fashionable, country club type of group with little interest in growth. The members didn't want to welcome people like this woman from "the wrong side of the tracks." They *certainly* didn't want her sitting next to some of the church's wealthiest members. So five times they denied her entrance and membership. The final time, one of the elders said to her, "Look, just go home and talk to God about it. Pray about it." She recognized that he was trying to brush her off, so she left.

They didn't hear from her for months. Then one day, that same elder went downtown to an office building where he saw this dear woman scrubbing floors. He recognized her and asked, "Aren't you the woman who tried to join our church?"

"I'm the very one," she replied.

"Did I encourage you to go home and have a talk with God?" he asked.

"Yes," she said, "you did."

"And did you have a talk with God?" he wondered.

She grinned and said, "Yes, I did."

"Really?" the man replied. "And what did God say?"

She looked up, smiled at the elder, and said, "The Lord told me not to be discouraged at all. He's been trying to get into your church for twenty years, with no more success than I've had."

We never want to become the kind of church where Jesus remains on the outside, trying to get in. It does happen! We often quote the famous passage in Revelation: *"Behold, I stand at the door and knock. If anyone hears My voice and opens the door, I will come in to him and dine with him"* (Revelation 3:20). While we usually quote the verse to unbelievers, in context, Jesus is speaking to His Church. It's a picture of Jesus standing outside of His own Church and calling out, "Excuse Me! Time out. This is supposed to be all about Me, but somehow it's become all about you." He was telling the *Church*, not unbelievers, to "open the door and let Me in."

Two Main Battles

Whenever we come to join a church or get actively involved in it, most of us face two main battles.

Number One: We battle our own preconceptions, our own ideas, our own traditional baggage of what church "ought to be."

"We've always done it that way!" we say. "I'm used to it that way, so that's the way it should be done." We battle our own traditions—yet many of them *must* be broken if we are to move ahead into the future God has for us.

Number Two: We battle our own culture. We live in a consumer-oriented culture driven by an egocentric, self-centered impulse. It's all about *us.*

People often approach church like they approach their own ego-centered culture. They go church shopping to find all the right ingredients "for me." I understand the motivation; I believe everybody does this, at least to some degree. The fundamental problem is the man-centered focus that drives it. It's all about *me*.

"What do they have to offer *me*? It has to make *me* feel good. *My* kids like this. Do they have a knitting class for *me*?" Totally absent is the real truth, namely, that "I exist for the glory and the purpose of Jesus Christ and what is best for *us* as a church."

A few years ago, a man walked up to me after a worship service and said, "We're shopping around for a church, and we're here today to see what you have to offer."

His words made me feel like an ingredient in a cake, as if I were a sack of flour sitting on a store shelf. Since he made his pronouncement in a fairly arrogant and curt way, I couldn't help but to respond as I did. "I appreciate that," I answered. "We're sure glad you're here. But can I just ask you a question? What do *you* have to offer?"

If you are going to be part of the church, then you are going to bring *something* to the table—some gift, some talent, or some involvement. The real question is never, "What can I get out of this place?" but rather, "What can I bring to this body?" Remember, it's all about *Him*.

The Early Church, Our Example

Acts 2 describes a landmark event. Everything that takes place afterward hinges on that single moment, the birth of the Church.

Here we see the church in its embryonic stage. It is growing, budding, and burgeoning—and it provides a firm pattern for us. It's our model, our grid, our example for answering the question, "How do we do church?" This is vitally important, because many people stop at some historical point and fail to go back far enough in time. They say, "We're a Reformation church . . . a Wesleyan church . . . a Moravian church." I say, "Keep going, buddy boy, all the way back to the very first model that God gave us." *That's* our example.

As we look closely at the Church of the early first century, we'll notice three main ingredients that marked it. If we are to have the same kind of spiritual success that it did, then we will have to follow the template it laid down almost two millennia ago.

Ingredient One: A Bold Proclamation of the Gospel

On the very first day of the infant Church, we see Peter in Jerusalem, boldly preaching the gospel. Crowds of Jewish people surround him, many of whom do not agree with his message. By and large, they reject the Messiah. Peter has come to the temple courts at the time of worship to say, *"Therefore let all the house of Israel know assuredly that God has made this Jesus, whom you crucified, both Lord and Christ"* (Acts 2:36).

Peter's message is direct, bold, packed with Scripture, and *very* convicting. His words pierced his listeners to the heart. They felt deeply convicted of their sins and they responded to this conviction with repentance. We could stop right here and write a whole chapter just on conviction of sin. How many times does the modern church preach a biblical message of repentance? Yet this was the church's very first public message after Pentecost. And Peter preached it boldly.

Before conversion, there must be conviction. Without conviction of sin, there can be no conversion. And before there is conviction, there must be proclamation. Somebody must have enough guts and love for Christ to boldly proclaim the gospel. That is the New Testament pattern, which never changes.

In Romans 10:14 Paul wrote, *"How then shall they call on Him in whom they have not believed? And how shall they believe in Him of whom they have not heard? And how shall they hear without a preacher?"*

Many of us like to talk about great revival and great salvation. Where do these great things come from?

Great salvation is *always* the result of great proclamation. Study any memorable revival or great movement of God in the past, and, at the very center, you will always find the bold proclamation of the gospel. This, then, must become the distinguishing mark of any church that claims to use the New Testament as its example.

If we say the New Testament gives us our marching orders, then we ought to be about evangelizing. I love an old quote by Oswald J. Smith: "The church that does not evangelize will fossilize." I've traveled the world and seen lots of churches on their way down, dying, and dead because they do everything *but* preach the gospel. Evangelism was the norm for the early church. Those first Christians told others about Jesus Christ; they simply couldn't help themselves.

Acts 4 describes how the word about Jesus got around: "*And with great power the apostles gave witness to the resurrection of the Lord Jesus*" (v. 33). In Acts 5, persecution followed the preaching of the gospel, and the religious authorities passed a law that banned the early Christians from preaching about Jesus in Jerusalem. So what did these first Christians do? "*Daily in the temple, and in every house, they did not cease teaching and preaching Jesus as the Christ*" (v. 42). By Acts 8, the persecution had grown much more severe, prompting many believers to flee Jerusalem and move out into Judea and Samaria. But they did not stop evangelizing: "*Therefore those who were scattered went everywhere preaching the word*" (v. 4). The hallmark of the early church was bold proclamation of the gospel.

"Yeah, Skip," someone might say, "but that was just the early days. *Of course* they were all excited. Jesus had just risen from the dead, people were being healed, and they saw signs and wonders. Everybody enjoyed this bandwagon effect. So sure, they felt excited and pumped up and eager to preach."

It was less exciting than you might think, mainly because of the intense danger involved. Since the religious authorities in Jerusalem wanted to stamp out this new movement as quickly as possible, they brought the apostles before the Jewish legal assembly, the Sanhedrin, pointed their fingers at Peter and John, and said, "It is now illegal for you to speak anymore in the name of Jesus Christ in this city."

And how did the apostles react? Immediately the church went to prayer:

> *And when they had prayed, the place where they were assembled together was shaken; and they were all filled with the Holy Spirit, and they spoke the word of God with boldness.* Acts 4:31

Once again we see a bold proclamation of the gospel.

Or consider a guy like Stephen. Religious officials brought him before the same ruling council that had threatened Peter and John—and for fifty long verses, Stephen gave a detailed account of Jewish history, from the call of Abraham until the death of Jesus Christ. Then he applied the lesson. And what a bold application he made!

> *"You stiff-necked and uncircumcised in heart and ears! You always resist the Holy Spirit; as your fathers did, so do you. Which of the prophets did your fathers not persecute? And they killed those who foretold the coming of the Just One, of whom you now have become the betrayers and murderers, who have received the law by the direction of angels and have not kept it."* Acts 7:51-53

There it is again: Stephen's listeners were "cut to the heart." But this group didn't ask him, "What shall we do?" as Peter's audience did. This group grabbed a bunch of rocks and pummeled Stephen with them until he died.

We see a similar pattern throughout the entire Book of Acts. In chapter 8, we see Philip visiting Samaria. And what did he do there? "[He] *preached Christ to them*" (Acts 8:5). In the very next chapter, we see Saul get saved on the way to Damascus; immediately thereafter he goes into the city and preaches the gospel that he had just been trying to stamp out. In the next chapter, Peter visits the house of Cornelius, a Roman, and there preaches the gospel. The rest of the book tells the story of Paul the apostle. Nobody could keep Paul from talking about Jesus. They threw him in jail, beat him, stoned him, left him for dead—and he'd keep getting up and walking to the next town, where once again he'd preach the gospel. Throughout the Book of Acts, there was *always* a bold proclamation of the gospel.

I will always treasure the memory of being in India and listening to two pastors discussing how big their churches had grown. When a veteran missionary came along, he heard them and said, "Brothers, when are you going to stop living in the Book of Numbers and start living in the Book of Acts?" If your church wants to live in the Book of Acts, then preach the gospel.

I doubt you'll find any dispute among genuine Christians that the gospel is precious. If you were to take a poll in any Bible-believing church, asking its members, "Do you love the gospel?" virtually everyone would say, "Yes, I love the gospel—the simple, old-time gospel. God sent His Son into the world to die for my sins!" But while all of us love it, far fewer seem to have a real desire to share it.

Not long ago the Barna Group found that only 55 percent of American born-again Christians had shared their faith with a non-believer during the previous year.[1] Quite often people come up with excuses for not sharing their faith. Some say they are scared, others say they are intimidated by tough questions, while others say that evangelism is not their gift.

I've discovered that evangelism isn't professional, but relational. You get to know people, you hang out with them, you work with them, then you share Jesus with them—it's natural. You explain the gospel to them because you love them enough to keep them out of hell. You want to see them with you in Heaven. Somebody said that the most selfish thing you can ever do is to feel content to go to Heaven alone. If you can get past that roadblock, then you'll become an evangelist.

Do people know *you* are a Christian? Remember the old Lady Clairol commercials: "Only her hairdresser knows

1. See Endnotes, page 249.

for sure." We have lots of Lady Clairol Christians out there—"Only God knows for sure"—because they never tell anyone.

You have to wonder why such a hesitance, a reluctance, a reticence to share the gospel? One reason for the timidity, I believe, comes from pulpits around this country. Many preachers seem ashamed of the gospel and embarrassed to mention the blood of Christ. Some churches today have pulled the plug on any song that refers to the blood of Jesus Christ. Do you know why? "It offends people," they say. A friend of mine used to serve as a worship leader. "Skip," he told me, "they won't even let me have too many songs that mention Jesus Christ in the worship service, let alone the blood of Christ."

I recently clipped a little newspaper advertisement from a church that boasted it embraced anyone and everyone: "We'll take you just the way you are. You don't have to change anything about yourself. If it's a barrier, we'll remove it." It sounds like a wonderful thing to say, doesn't it? But here is my question: "What if the *gospel* is a barrier? Will you remove that too?" A lot of places today respond, "Yes."

I agree with British pundit G. K. Chesterton who once said, "We do not want a church that will move with the world; we want a church that will move the world." The church described in Acts rocked its world. Why? Because its members chose to make a bold proclamation of the gospel.

Ingredient Two: A Glad Reception

Any church that takes the Book of Acts as its example will boldly proclaim the gospel—and then it will stand back and watch, thrilled, as God brings a glad reception:

> *Then those who gladly received his word were baptized; and that day about three thousand souls were added to them.* Acts 2:41

Have you ever tried to picture this scene? Can you imagine what Peter might have thought? I don't know exactly how he brought the crowd to a point of decision, but I doubt he did it the way I do it. Still, I wonder if he said, "Now, as we keep our heads bowed and our eyes closed, is there anybody here in the temple courts who would like to receive Christ? Just raise your hand." When he looked up, he saw 3,000 hands. *WOW! This is magnificent!* That's astronomical growth!

Luke writes that the people "gladly received his word." You could translate that phrase, "they joyfully welcomed it" or, "they consented to it" or even, "they gave his word entrance."

What does a church need if it is to grow? First, it needs "scattering hands." That's evangelism. You take the seed of the gospel and you throw it everywhere you go: in the supermarket, with your friends, at work, at home, and in the neighborhood. But a growing church also needs something else. Second, the church needs "listening ears," as in Acts 2. The people gladly received Peter's message. Faith comes by hearing and hearing by the Word of God. Tremendous growth takes place simply by listening intently to the Word of God.

So—how are you hearing?

"Well, Skip," someone says, "I'm hearing just fine; thanks for asking. I don't have a hearing problem." No, that's not what I mean. I mean, how are you *listening*?

"What do you mean, *how am I listening*? I don't understand."

Jesus put it like this: *"Therefore take heed how you hear"* (Luke 8:18). In other words, "Be very careful how you process the information coming to you through your ears." Immediately after He said these words, Jesus told His listeners, *"For whoever has, to him more will be given; and whoever does not have, even what he seems to have will be taken from him."* No wonder some people have been in church their whole lives and still say, "I don't get it"!

"He who has ears to hear," Jesus often said, "let him hear!" (See Mark 4:9, 23; Luke 8:8; 14:35). Do *you* have ears to hear?

A person can listen actively or passively. When you listen passively, you put your brain in neutral—like how most of us watch television. We have no intention of applying what we hear or allowing ourselves to be changed by it. Instead, we grade it: "On a scale of one to ten, I'd give it a six—easy to dance to, nice listening, but a little too loud." That's passive listening, mechanical listening.

On the other hand, you can listen actively. That means you come with a very different attitude: "I have an appointment with God today. God is going to speak to me through His Word, and I want to listen to Him very carefully, even take down a few notes. I'll pray about them when I go home. I'm going to *really* listen, because God wants to communicate something special to me."

Hebrews 2:1 says, *"Therefore we must give the more earnest heed to the things we have heard, lest we drift away."* A crucial message needs attentive listeners—and we see such listeners throughout the Bible.

Ezra the scribe had a *great* audience. When he gave a message that lasted at least four hours, his audience stayed with him the whole way: *"Then he read from it* [the Scripture] *in the open square that was in front of the Water Gate from morning until midday, before the men and women and those who could understand; and the ears of all the people were attentive to the Book of the Law"* (Nehemiah 8:3).

Paul preached to the Thessalonians and later wrote to them, *"You became followers of us and of the Lord, having received the word in much affliction, with joy of the Holy Spirit"* (1 Thessalonians 1:6). In other words, "I know your outward circumstances were tough when I gave you the message, but you accepted it and pondered it and took it into yourselves with great joy." His message had a glad reception in the hearts of the Thessalonians.

God loves to use the bold preaching of the Word to bring joy to the hearts of those who receive that Word, as the Philippian jailer discovered: *"He was filled with joy because he had come to believe in God—he and his whole family"* (Acts 16:34, NIV).

Ingredient Three: A Steadfast Dedication

When any church adds a third ingredient—steadfast dedication—to a bold preaching of the gospel and to a joyful reception of that message, the result can be explosive. Consider what happened as Peter wrapped up his first sermon after Pentecost:

And with many other words he testified and exhorted them, saying,

> *"Be saved from this perverse generation." Then those who gladly received his word were baptized; and that day about three thousand souls were added to them. And they* [that is, the 3,000 new baby believers] *continued steadfastly in the apostles' doctrine and fellowship, in the breaking of bread, and in prayers.*

> *Then fear came upon every soul, and many wonders and signs were done through the apostles.*
> Acts 2:40-43

The words "continued steadfastly" come from a single word in Greek, *proskartereo*. This term means "to adhere to" or "to stick to something with great strength." To "continue steadfastly," then, means "to be earnest toward" or "to be constantly diligent." This new group of believers had a passion and a spiritual excitement to grow in the Lord.

The same word appears in verse 46, although in a different verbal form: *"So continuing daily with one accord in the temple."* The word translated "continuing" comes from the same Greek term, *proskartereo*. The verb tense here suggests an ongoing process of firm dedication: "I'm not going to quit. I'm not going to give up. I'm here to stay. I'm going to stick it out, regardless of what comes."

Jesus himself employed another term, which sums it all up. He instructed us to "abide" in Him (see John 15:4). The Greek term translated "abide" (*meno*) means "to remain" or "to maintain a constant, living communion." Jesus means whoever "abides" or "remains" in Him enjoys a constant, living communion. Those who exhibit a steadfast dedication to Him grow in grace and become mighty tools in His hands.

Members of this first church were saved, listening, and had dedicated themselves to each other in their new community of faith. They remained steadfast in the apostles' doctrine, they remained steadfast in fellowship, they remained steadfast in the breaking of bread, and they remained steadfast in their prayer life.

Although we probably wouldn't consider these 3,000 brand-new believers mature—after all, they had just gotten saved—they were dedicated. And that dedication made a *huge* difference. These brand-new Christians stuck with it.

They didn't walk forward, shed a tear, say a little prayer, and then say, "Hey, what's next?" and move away and forget about church. They remained steadfastly dedicated to their Lord and to the church He founded.

If we want to successfully follow their lead, we'll again have to battle our culture. We live in a very transient society; a full 20 percent of this nation's population moves *every year*. Because we often approach the church culture as we approach the American culture, we think it's just fine to keep moving from church to church as well. "I'll be in this church a little while," we say, "and then maybe try that church for a period." We shop around and hop from church to church.

You can go ahead and follow that pattern if you want—but you won't find happiness anywhere you go. You'll never feel happy with *any* church, *ever*, because you've made it all about *you*. Contrast that with the new believers of Acts 2. Here we encounter a group of steadfast, dedicated, faithful people.

One preacher said to his congregation, "All that I ask is that we apply the same standard of faithfulness to our church activities that we would in other areas of life. The church, after all, is concerned about faithfulness. Consider these examples: If your car started one out of three times, would you consider it faithful? If you didn't show up at work two or three times a month, would your boss call you faithful? If you miss a couple of mortgage payments in a year's time, would the mortgage holder say, 'Oh well, ten out of twelve isn't bad'? If you attend worship meetings only often enough to show you're interested—but not enough to get involved—are you faithful?"[2] How about you? Are you faithful to your local church body and an example of

---

2. See Endnotes, page 249.

steadfast dedication? Could it be said of you, as Paul said of Timothy, *"I have no one like-minded, who will sincerely care for your state. For all seek their own, not the things which are of Christ Jesus. But you know his proven character, that as a son with his father he served with me in the gospel"* (Philippians 2:20-22). Are you a modern-day Timothy? You can be, if you want to be. All it takes is a choice.

Let's Help Jesus Build His Church

The New Testament church is our pattern. The first century Church, under the headship of Christ, wrote the course material for "Church-building 101."

And what was the early church? It was a group of saved people who loved and practiced evangelism wherever they went. It was a congregation of redeemed men and women who listened carefully to the Word and received it gladly. They gladly received the truth and had an abiding commitment to the new fellowship they joined.

This is the kind of church that Jesus loves to be a part of. He is not standing on the outside, knocking, and saying, "Time out! May I come in?" And *this* is the kind of church that Jesus wants to build—a Christ-centered body that works eagerly to bring more and more people to faith in Him.

So, is organization important? Yes. Is doctrine important? Yes. Are the many groups that spring out of a fellowship important? Yes. Is it important that you get involved? It always is—but all to the glory of God. *It must always be about Him.*

A little boy who had just moved with his family to a new town went to Sunday school class for the first time. He wondered how he would like his new class. When he approached his mom afterwards, she asked him, "Well, how was it?"

"It was *great*," he said, beaming, "I loved it."

"And what did you learn?" his mom asked. The little boy told her all about the lesson, and then his mom asked, "And what's your Sunday school teacher's name?"

The little boy looked down, furrowed his brow, and after a moment said, "I can't remember her name—but she must have been Jesus' grandmother because she couldn't talk about anybody else!"

May such an observation mark *us* as we seek to partner with Jesus to build His Church.

CHAPTER 8

The Top
OF THE LIST

Several years ago Richard Lederer compiled a list of Bible stories as retold by students around the country. His work made it into *National Review*. If you want to know what the Bible says about creating the right conditions for a church to grow, *don't* pay any attention to what follows.

- "Guinnesses" is the first book of the Bible.
- God got tired of creating the world, so He took the Sabbath off.
- Adam and Eve were created from an apple tree.
- Noah's wife was called Joan of Ark.
- Lot's wife was a pillar of salt by day, but a ball of fire by night.
- Samson slayed the Philistines with the axe of the apostles.
- Moses went up on Mount Cyanide to get the Ten Amendments.
- The First Commandment is when Eve told Adam to eat the apple; the Fifth Commandment is humor thy father and mother; the Seventh Commandment is thou shalt not admit adultery.

- Moses died before he ever reached Canada.
- Joshua led the Hebrews in the battle of Geritol.
- Solomon, one of David's sons, had 300 wives and 700 porcupines.
- Jesus was born because Mary had an immaculate contraption.
- The people who followed the Lord were called the 12 decibels.
- A Christian should have only one wife; this is called monotony.[1]

So where should you look if you *do* want to investigate the Bible's principles for growing a strong, healthy church? In the next four chapters, I'd like to revisit the second chapter of Acts and there identify the four top priorities of the early church. Let's ask ourselves, "What key activities marked them, bound them together, and equipped them to succeed in very difficult circumstances?"

Priority One: The Apostles' Doctrine

Note very carefully what landed as Number One on the priority list of the early church: "*And they continued steadfastly in the apostles' doctrine*" (Acts 2:42).

I think it's both crucial and vital that "the apostles' doctrine" is first on the priority list of the early church. It's not second, third, or fourth, but first. It's Number One, at the top of the order. Luke didn't write, "And they continued steadfastly in singing and praying." He didn't report, "They continued steadfastly in loving each other." While loving, singing, doing missions, and all the rest are vital for any growing church, none appear first on the list.

1. See Endnotes, page 249.

And why not? Why should doctrine be first on the list? It turns out there's a very simple reason. Unless you know the apostles' doctrine, you won't know how to love, do missions, have fellowship, or accomplish anything else worthwhile in the Christian community. Without focusing first on the apostles' doctrine, you'll either overemphasize or underemphasize something, and soon things in your church will become chaotic and dysfunctional.

Emphasizing the apostles' doctrine—that is, putting all of the Scriptures together and discovering God's mind through the Word—enables us to perform all of the necessary church functions in the right way. It brings harmony and balance to our lives.

This is one reason why, in my preaching, I am committed to working my way from the beginning of one book of the Bible all the way through to the end. It's why I begin with Genesis and proceed all the way to Revelation. When you work your way through the Bible like this, you discover every single issue God considers important, you get it in context, and you get it with the emphasis God gives it. That's beautiful!

When somebody says to me, "You ought to talk more about the family," I tend to respond, "I will, once we get to it in the Bible." It's in there, even though it might not be mentioned on every page.

Or when someone asks me, "When are you going to speak about finances?" I usually say, "We'll get to it. The Bible has a lot to say about finances."

It's funny, but in all the years I've been preaching, no one has ever said, "Why don't you speak more on tithing?" I know some preachers think tithing is on every page of the Bible. It's not, but it's definitely in there, and I think it's best to speak of it in its context.

The point is, when you preach through the Bible in this way, you come to every topic that God sees as important, as well as the emphasis that God gives to every topic.

Paul trained quite a few pastors, including Timothy, whom he left at Ephesus to raise up that church. The first letter of Paul to Timothy is all about church order: bishops, elders, deacons, women in the church, men in the church, how believers ought to act whenever they gather. It also speaks a great deal about doctrine. In fact, Paul writes, "*Till I come, give attention to reading, to exhortation, to doctrine*" (1 Timothy 4:13).

In his Second Letter to Timothy, Paul identifies the young preacher's main priority in ministry—and he also explains why it should come first. When you consider that 2 Timothy was the last letter Paul ever wrote, his words reveal something very significant:

> *I charge you therefore before God and the Lord Jesus Christ, who will judge the living and the dead at His appearing and His kingdom:*
>
> *Preach the word! Be ready in season and out of season. Convince, rebuke, exhort, with all longsuffering and teaching* [or "doctrine"].
>
> *For the time will come when they will not endure sound doctrine, but according to their own desires, because they have itching ears, they will heap up for themselves teachers; and they will turn their ears away from the truth, and be turned aside to fables.*
> 2 Timothy 4:1-4

I find this remarkable. Paul says that a time is coming when the church, even those who profess to be Christians, won't endure sound doctrine. They'll listen only to what they want to hear—to whatever tickles their fancy, no matter how distant from the truth of God—and they'll flock to any teacher who promises to tell them whatever most appeals to their lusts.

A recent article by The Barna Group revealed statistics that might shock you. According to the article, author and researcher George Barna found that only 7 percent of the nation's Protestants have a biblical worldview. He defined this worldview as a belief in biblically-based absolute moral truth in addition to six fundamental biblical beliefs: "The accuracy of biblical teaching, the sinless nature of Jesus, the literal existence of Satan, the omnipotence and omniscience of God, salvation by grace alone, and the personal responsibility to evangelize." Upon further research, a national survey found that only half, or rather 51 percent, of the nation's Protestant pastors have a biblical worldview. As a result of his research, Barna states:

The most important point is that you can't give people what you don't have. The low percentage of Christians who have a biblical worldview is a direct reflection of the fact that half of our primary religious teachers and leaders do not have one. In some denominations, the vast majority of clergy do not have a biblical worldview, and it shows up clearly in the data related to the theological views and moral choices of people who attend those churches.[2] I would say to these pastors, "What are you doing in the ministry? What are you doing behind a pulpit? What *do* you believe in? Why do you bother with ministry at all?"

"The time is coming when they will not endure sound doctrine," Paul said, "so Timothy, make doctrine your top priority. Preach the Word! Don't preach your opinions or 'feel good' talks. Preach and teach the Word of God, the apostles' doctrine."

---

2. See Endnotes, page 249.

Already you can visit some churches and hear trimmed-down sermons (fifteen minutes, tops) with longer sets of music and drama—and nobody minds. In fact, they applaud it. But if someone should dare to do an expository message—which means taking out some of the other stuff in order to lengthen the sermon—it simply will not be tolerated. "They will not endure sound doctrine," Paul warns.

One evening a few years ago, when my son Nathan was growing up, my wife had prepared a beautiful meal, including asparagus. You know how a little boy feels about things like asparagus, don't you? To him it's like brussels sprouts or broccoli—*yuck*! But he had to eat it. I wanted to say, "Honey, just let him have whatever he wants; he's a boy, for crying out loud." But I didn't say it (I was wise enough to keep my mouth shut).

We had muffins with jam at the end of the table. Nathan's eyes remained glued to the muffins and hardly noticed the asparagus. The deal was, however, that if he wanted the muffins, then he had to eat the asparagus. He might not have liked vegetables as much as he liked pastry, but we knew that veggies were a whole lot more necessary to his health.

A lot of Christians will not endure sound asparagus. They want the jam and the buttered up cakes, but not the vegetables. Yet if their pastor does not help them endure sound doctrine and develop an appetite for it, their desires will ruin them. I know I consider it a wasted day if I am not, in some way, enriched by the Word of God and fortified by something that the Lord speaks to me from the Scriptures.

"The apostles' doctrine" has to remain at the top of our list!

Doctrine: Its Definition

Okay, so "the apostles' doctrine" needs to remain first on the church's priority list. But what exactly does "the apostles' doctrine" mean? To what does it refer?

If you were to check a Bible concordance and count how many times the word "doctrine" appears in the New Testament, you'd discover that it shows up thirty-seven times. Now, when any term appears that often, you can assume that it carries some significant weight. It's important. The underlying Greek term here is *didache*, which means "teaching" or "instruction." The early disciples continually devoted themselves to the apostles' instruction and teaching.

In the last few years, the word "doctrine" has gotten a bad rap. You can just hear the moaning: "Oh no— we're going to talk *doctrine*!" Over the years I've heard this complaint countless times, even in subtle ways. Sometimes I overhear informal conversations: "Well, we're not really into doctrine here. Doctrine isn't all that important. All we do is love each other and accept each other. We put doctrine aside."

Can you hear how ludicrous that sounds? "We don't care about teaching here. We don't care about instruction. We don't care about truth. All we want to do is love each other. We put truth and teaching and instruction aside."

I love gadgets. There is only one catch: I hate the manuals that come with the gadgets. I almost never read them. The manual is so much bigger than the gadget! I'm not going to read that thing. I'm going to figure it out on my own. I'm going to turn it on, study it, and get it licked. And if it breaks, I can call somebody who knows how to make it work.

But what happens when the gadget breaks and I *can't* find anybody who can help me fix it? What then? My last resort is to get out the manual.

That's my fear—that a lot of us believers live our Christian lives by the seat of our pants. We try to figure things out on our own, as we go, and when it all breaks down, *then* we want to know what the manual of life (the Bible) says about how we are to live. So we neglect the Word of God and do not give it the priority it enjoyed in the early church. That's my chief concern: Many of us who call ourselves Christian seem more concerned about how we feel about some issue than about what God's Word says.

James Montgomery Boice was an influential Presbyterian pastor in Philadelphia who is now in Heaven. He wrote, "We do not have a strong church today, nor do we have many strong Christians. We can trace the cause to an acute lack of sound spiritual knowledge....Ask an average Christian to talk about God. After getting past the expected answers you will find that his god is a little god of vacillating sentiments."[3]

Remember what the prophet Hosea said about the spiritual condition of his own day? As he considered the spiritual landscape of his nation, he said, "*My people are destroyed for lack of knowledge*" (Hosea 4:6). Everywhere he looked, Hosea saw his countrymen acting in foolish, destructive ways that invited the judgment of God to fall on them—and all because they refused to listen to what God wanted to tell them through His Word. When it comes to Bible truth, ignorance is not bliss; in fact, it's devastating.

I had a pastor friend who for a long time taught the Bible in his church. Then one day he thought, *I don't want to do just this all my life; I want to have a little fun.* So he

3. See Endnotes, page 249.

pushed the Bible aside and did just about everything else in his services. When the whole thing came crashing down, he made an interesting confession to me. "Skip," he said, "I have to confess that my church is biblically illiterate—and I'm responsible."

I think about Jesus' own day and about the crowds that came to listen to Him. On four separate occasions, He asked the religious leaders of His time, almost with incredulity, "Have you not read?" (See Matthew 12:3, 5; 19:4; 22:31.) In other words, "Don't you guys read your Bibles? Don't you know the doctrines laid out in God's Word?"

At least four times in his own letters, the Apostle Paul told his audiences some version of, "I do not want you to be ignorant, brethren, concerning . . ." (See Romans 11:25; 1 Corinthians 10:1; 12:1; 1 Thessalonians 4:13.) What's interesting is that three of the things he refers to are: (1) spiritual gifts, (2) the blindness of Israel, and (3) the Second Coming of Christ. To me this is fascinating because these are the same three areas where I find today's Christians are most ignorant. But Paul specifically said, "I don't *want* you to be ignorant. [You need knowledge in these areas]."

Paul trained young pastors like Timothy and Titus and then sent them into churches like Ephesus and Crete. And whenever he dispatched these young pastors to their new assignments, he instructed them to keep the Word of God as a top priority in their ministries.

In 1636, just sixteen years after the pilgrims landed at Plymouth Rock, the very first American college opened its doors, and it was named after a preacher. The preacher's name was John Harvard. Does that ring a bell? Eventually, the school became Harvard University.

Long ago, Harvard University departed from its original mission. Colonists had founded the college to train clergymen. They wanted to be sure the gospel and the Word of God remained preeminent—and here's why: "[We are] dreading to leave an illiterate ministry to the churches, when our present ministers shall lie in the dust."[4]

I compare my job as a pastor to a mom in a kitchen. My own mom used to say, "I slave over a hot stove all day long for you kids." Do you remember hearing your mom say anything like that?

As a pastor, I go into the spiritual kitchen and slave over a hot stove during the week to make sure that when we gather, we all have a solid meal to enjoy. I ask myself, "Why would people get up early on a Sunday morning and come to church?" I have to make sure that we have something nutritious to eat and that it's ready for the table. That's why we plow deeply through Scripture and look carefully into context, history, background, word usage, and all the rest. It's all necessary if we are to lay a solid foundation.

I wonder—how do you fare in conversation when the Bible comes up? When people in a crowd or at the office say things like, "There are so many contradictions in the Bible," or, "What does the Bible mean when it says . . . ", how do you respond? Or when a cultist knocks at your door and says, "Hi, I'm one of Jehovah's Christian Witnesses. You know, Jesus is not God—where do you get that idea?" How do you reply? Do you give biblical answers to people with questions?

That's a good definition of doctrine: *biblical answers for people who have questions.* Again, it comes back to sound instruction or healthy teaching. When the early church gathered, God's people listened to the apostles teach from the Word of God. They formed an alliance based on the

4. See Endnotes, page 249.

apostles' doctrine—their teaching, their instruction—that was sound, healthy, and spiritually nourishing.

Doctrine: Its Designation

The early church didn't gather to hear any old doctrine; Luke says they met to hear "the apostles' doctrine." They didn't come together to hear nice thoughts or some scholar's latest opinions; they came to drink in the apostles' doctrine.

And what, exactly, does that mean? How does the apostles' doctrine differ from any other form of doctrine? If we take a closer look at the context, I think we'll get the idea.

The Church was born on the day of Pentecost, one of the three annual feasts that pious Jews had to attend if they lived anywhere near Judah. They were expected to make a pilgrimage to the Temple and worship with other pilgrims. Most people did this in caravans. Once they arrived, they lived in small, temporary shelters and worshiped at the Feast of Passover. Then, if they had traveled a great distance, many would stay an extra fifty days until the Feast of Pentecost rolled around.

On this day, the Feast of Pentecost, Peter preached the gospel in the temple courts to Jews from around the world—and 3,000 worshipers got saved. Picture it! From a little church of 120 members (that's how many had gathered in an upper room), Christ's body grew twenty-five times larger *in one day*. What would *you* do with them all?

You'd train them, as the early church did. There were twelve apostles (including Judas's replacement); 120 believers; 3,000 new converts; and then more men and women who got saved every day. That means that every one of the apostles could have an assembly of about 300 people.

And what would you teach them? As Jews, this crowd of 3,000 new believers all had a spiritual background. They knew the Old Testament Scriptures. That was their Bible, and that's why Peter reached back into the Old Testament to quote Joel and Psalm 16 to show that Jesus Christ really was the promised Messiah. All of it—the death, burial, and Resurrection of Jesus—had been predicted.

That's the apostles' doctrine. It's simply the apostles explaining how the Old Testament Scriptures were fulfilled in the Messiah's death, burial, and resurrection. Like a lawyer laying down his case, Peter showed how all of the Old Testament's prophecies concerning the Messiah came together in Christ. He went back to Moses, David, and various prophets to demonstrate how Jesus fulfilled them all. And the people responded! From that point on, they couldn't get enough of the apostles' doctrine.

A recent poll revealed that at least one copy of the Bible can be found in 92 percent of all American households; however, only 59 percent of Americans said they actually read the Bible once in a while and even less, only 37 percent, said they read it once a week. Many say they revere the Bible, but significantly less actually revere it through reading.[5] What a change from the time of the apostles to our society today! The members of the early church devoted themselves steadfastly to the apostles' doctrine; we don't.

We need to follow the example of the prophet Jeremiah, who said to the Lord about the Bible, "*Your words were found, and I ate them, and Your word was to me the joy and rejoicing of my heart*" (Jeremiah 15:16). Do you love to "find" and "eat" God's words? Is His Word the joy and

---

5. See Endnotes, page 249.

rejoicing of your heart? Because the early church devoted itself to the apostles' doctrine, it turned the ancient world on its head.

"Well, my church reads the Bible," someone says. But recognize the enormous difference between any old teaching and "the apostles' doctrine." Many preachers begin their sermons with a Scripture text—but they don't stick with it. They start with a text, depart from the text, and never return to the text. Their method ends up being a short talk for Christians rather than an expositional teaching of the apostles' doctrine.

One of my favorite texts is Luke 24. It describes what happened after the death, burial, and Resurrection of Jesus Christ. The two disciples of Luke 24 don't know that Jesus has risen from the dead, so they are very sad. As they walk down the road, they feel very bummed out. Their heads are down, they're shuffling their feet, they're talking quietly to one another about the recent tragedy—and then Jesus comes walking up to them, incognito. They have no idea it's Him (which, apparently, He likes). Soon He starts asking them questions.

"Why are you guys so bummed out?"

They turn to Jesus, still not recognizing Him, and say, "What? Are you a stranger around here? Don't you know the things that have happened here lately?"

"What things?" Jesus answers. Classic! The events that so discouraged them had everything to do with Him, but He plays it as if He has no idea. He wants to hear the story from them.

And so they tell Him about this Jesus of Nazareth character. "We had hoped that He was going to be the Messiah, but He's dead. That's why we're so bummed."

The Bible says that Jesus looked at them and said, "*O foolish ones, and slow of heart to believe in all that the prophets have spoken! Ought not the Christ to have suffered these things and to enter into His glory?*" (Luke 24:25-26). And then Luke adds, "*And beginning at Moses and all the Prophets, He expounded to them in all the Scriptures the things concerning Himself*" (v. 27).

Man, if ever there were a Bible study that I wish had been recorded, that's it! I would *love* to hear that message. Jesus reached back through the Old Testament and showed them how all of its predictions in the Psalms, in the Law, and in the Prophets actually referenced himself.

As the story continues, Jesus acts as though He wants to travel further, but they beg Him to stay. They invite Him to share a meal, which He does. When He blesses and breaks the bread, at last they recognize Him—and He vanishes out of their sight. One astonished friend turns toward the other and says, "*Did not our heart burn within us while He talked with us on the road, and while He opened the Scriptures to us?*" (Luke 24:32).

I love that—they had spiritual heartburn! They were talking about a spiritual sensation crackling in their hearts, filling them with hope and wonder.

Don't miss *why* their hearts burned. "Didn't our hearts burn," they said, "*while He opened the Scriptures to us?*"

This kind of spiritual burning sensation comes from a new understanding of familiar things. Jesus didn't speak a *new* word of God to them. He spoke to them of passages that had existed for many hundreds of years. He began in Moses and all the Prophets and expounded certain texts. These men had grown up in the Scriptures. As devout Jews, they had heard the Bible all their lives. Jesus simply gave them a new application of the old revelation.

I hear a lot Christians say things like, "I need a new experience. I need new revelation." No, you don't. You need a fresh application of the old stuff. That's all. When the old revelation gets unlocked in your heart and released in your mind—when you start to see Christ in it and thus understand its true significance—then it will set your heart on fire. You'll be able to say, "My heart burned! He talked to me in His Word, in the apostles' doctrine, and He opened up the Scriptures to me." When that happens, everything changes.

Doctrine: Their Devotion to It

The members of the early church "devoted" themselves to the apostles' doctrine. That is, they loved hearing it. They couldn't get enough of it. They met often just so they could listen to God speak to them from His Word and so learn how they were to be His witnesses to the world.

If you gave them a choice between a T-bone steak and the meat of the Word, they'd choose the Word.

I have to tell you, this kind of love for the apostles' doctrine is not automatic; it has to be cultivated. It is *not* part of our fallen human nature. We naturally say, "Are we done yet? Is the sermon over yet? I have to get some lunch. I have some important things to do. When can I get out of here?"

So how can we cultivate a love and a devotion to the Scriptures, as the early church had? Allow me to make a few suggestions.

1. Carry a Bible.

I have a Bible in my car, another one in my motorcycle saddlebag, and a third one in a golf bag—even though I rarely play golf. I want to make sure that I'll have at least one thing I know how to do when I'm on the golf course (that's how bad I am).

A friend of mine has the Bible on his PDA. When I asked him what he does with it, he replied, "A lot of times when you are in gridlock or you're in a doctor's office, you can't do anything but sit and wait. I like to have the Word with me at those times."

2. *Bring your Bible to church.*

I know that a lot of churches project the highlighted Scripture text on a screen, but there is something about finding the verse or passage for yourself in your own Bible and reading it along with everyone else that cements it in your memory. At a later time of need, you're more likely to be able to find it and profit from it.

3. *Bring a notebook and take notes.*

When you combine writing with listening, you increase both your comprehension and your retention of what you hear. Make it a habit to write down the main points of a sermon, as well as any cross-references listed. When you get home, look up the other passages and see how the Lord might apply them to your life.

4. *Meditate on the Word of God.*

Forget everything the world has told you about meditation, transcendental or otherwise. Biblical meditation simply means to focus your attention and thoughts on one text for a period of time. It's hard to do because we live in a very distracted society. We get barraged by stuff all the time, so to sit and think about one thing over an extended period of time is hard—but enriching.

I've been to India several times, and every time I go it strikes me how many crazed "holy men" you see sitting around, meditating in trances for hours, with various pins and rods and other painful things stuck through various parts of their bodies. And I think, *Here they are meditating on that worthless stuff—and Christians somehow can't find the time to meditate on the Word of God, the eternal truth from Heaven?* "*Consider what I say,*" Paul writes, "*and may the Lord give you understanding in all things*" (2 Timothy 2:7).

5. *Tell somebody what you've learned.*

Whenever you learn something in your quiet time, through a message, in a radio program, or from a book, call a friend and tell him or her the insight you've received. That will whet your appetite for the next step, which is becoming a teacher. If you want to *really* learn something, then teach it. That's why I love to teach the Bible; I learn so much in my studies.

6. *Memorize the Bible.*

I don't mean you need to commit all of the Word to memory, although I know some people who are making that their aim; they've already memorized several books of the Bible. Start by memorizing a verse or two at a time. As the Psalmist said, "*Your word I have hidden in my heart, that I might not sin against You*" (Psalm 119:11). Commit well-chosen portions of the Bible to memory, because in a time of crisis—let's say, when somebody bumps into you—what will spill out is what you've brought into your mind and heart.

7. *Look for other places to study the Bible.*

Do not confine your Bible study to a Sunday morning worship experience. Get involved with a Bible study group, or look for other opportunities to study the Word, as in a Wednesday night Bible study at church. Learn to plow through Scripture verse-by-verse, chapter-by-chapter, all the way through the Bible. "Oh, but I'm so busy," you say. Aren't we all? If you want to experience the spiritual success and joy that characterized the early church, then change your schedule and make it a priority to study the Word of God.

Let the psalmist be your teacher: *"I will delight myself in Your statutes; I will not forget Your word"* (Psalm 119:16).

Treat It As a Love Letter

Have you ever been in love? If so, you remember the love letters. Somewhere, my wife and I still have the love letters we wrote to each other during our dating days.

I clearly remember going to the mailbox and seeing a letter from Lenya. Let me tell you, I treated that letter differently from any other thing in my mailbox! I did not say, "Oh, another one from her," as though it were a bill or some junk mail. I felt excited to see it; I tore it open and I hung on every word.

An item in the *New York Times* titled, "How to Read a Love Letter," pictures an adolescent receiving a love letter and poring over the words:

This young man just received his first love letter. He may have read it already three or four times, but he is just beginning. To read it as accurately as he would like would require several dictionaries and a good deal of close work with a few experts in etymology and philology. However, he'll do all right without them. He will ponder over the exact shade of the meaning of every word, every comma.

And she has headed the letter, "Dear John." "What," he asks himself, "is the significance of those words?" Did she refrain from saying Dearest [his name was John; it was not a "Dear John" letter] because she was bashful?

Would "my dear" have sounded too formal? Jeepers, maybe she would have said, "Dear so and so," to anybody. A worried frown appears on his face.

But it disappears as soon as he really gets to think about it.

He thinks about the first sentence. "She certainly wouldn't have said *that* to just anybody." So he works his way through the letter, one moment perched blissfully on a cloud, the next moment huddled miserable behind an eight ball. It has started a hundred questions in his mind. He could now quote it by heart; in fact, he will, to himself, for weeks to come.

At the end of this story, the author remarked that we would be a race of literary giants, if only we would read books like this boy read that letter. We really would, wouldn't we? And that makes me wonder: What if Christians read the Bible like this boy read his love letter? Why, we'd become a race of *spiritual* giants!

Through His Word, God wants to speak to you and to me. The members of the early church understood this; that's why they dedicated themselves to the apostles' doctrine. They put it, in fact, at the top of their priority list.

Where is it on yours?

CHAPTER 9

What No TV

CAN GIVE YOU

An article in the *New York Times* titled, "Social Ties Reduce Risk of a Cold," reports how involvement with others is good for our health. The articles states:

Building on a dozen studies correlating friendship and fellowship with health, a new study has found that people with a broad array of social

ties are significantly less likely to catch colds than those with sparse social networks. The incidence of infection among people who knew many different kinds of people was nearly half that among those who were relatively isolated . . . The lack of diverse social contacts was the strongest of the risk factors for colds that were examined, including smoking, low vitamin C intake and stress.[1]

Some people believe that isolation will render them healthy, keeping them free from germs, but it appears that isolation does quite the opposite, leaving their immune systems weaker and their bodies more susceptible to illness.

1. See Endnotes, page 249.

In the same way that isolation is not good for the human body, it is not good for the body that is the Church.

The fact is, God made all of us with the desire and the need for close relationships. He designed and built us with relationships in mind. And some of the most significant relationships we can have, He intends for us to find in church.

Priority Two: The Fellowship

Acts 2:42 says, "*And they continued steadfastly in the apostles' doctrine* and fellowship . . . " (emphasis added). The early church was a learning church; they devoted themselves to the apostles' doctrine. But it was also a loving church; they continued steadfastly in fellowship. Fellowship appears second on the list, right after the apostles' doctrine.

The second priority of fellowship balances out the first one of the apostles' doctrine, and here's how. If the church is *only* about Bible teaching and the apostles' doctrine, then it can become cold and academic. If, on the other hand, the church is concerned *only* about fellowship, then it can become just a social club. But if the fellowship centers around the apostles' doctrine, then it can become dynamic—and that's just what we want.

What Is "The Fellowship"?

Before we can consider how to achieve great fellowship, first we had better know what it is. If you know any words from the Greek New Testament, you probably know the term *agape*, love. You hear it all the time. Perhaps you also recognize a second Greek term: *koinonia*. Just about every Christian has heard that word, even though it's from the Greek language.

Koinonia means "fellowship." In Acts 2:42, a definite article appears in front of it: *ha koinonia*, "the fellowship"—which means the early church enjoyed a special kind of fellowship. That's important to know because a lot of people tack the word "fellowship" onto just about any Christian gathering. "Fellowship" really doesn't mean, "I hang out in Jesus' name." By the way, this verse makes no mention of coffee and donuts.

The term *koinonia* is often translated "fellowship," but in other contexts we see it rendered "communion" or "distribution" or "contribution" and even "partnership." Now, ponder for a moment the various ways the term is used. You can never "do" fellowship by yourself. You can't say, "I'll just stay at home and enjoy some good fellowship by myself." To have fellowship, you must have people around you.

After one Sunday service a lady told me, "I talked to a friend who belonged to an interesting church. When I asked where she fellowshiped, she replied, 'The Bedside Baptist Fellowship. I lie in bed every Sunday and turn on the television, or I listen to the radio. That's my church.'"

I'm sorry, but *koinonia* just doesn't work that way. *Koinonia* was one of the four major priorities of the early church. You can certainly stay home and listen to a worship service on the radio or watch one on television, but by doing so you're certainly not "in church." You might be hearing good music or listening to a wonderful sermon, but what you have is very far from a substitute for church.

Koinonia denotes being together, interacting with one another. In his book *People-Centered Evangelism*, John Havlik writes, "The church is never a place, but always a people; never a fold but always a flock; never a sacred building but always a believing assembly. The church is you who pray, not where you pray. A structure of brick or marble can no more be the church than your clothes of serge or satin can be you. There is in this world nothing sacred but man, no sanctuary of man but the soul."[2]

Certainly the early church was devoted to the fellowship. They regularly got together with one another. But why? For what purpose? Principally, they met to stimulate each other to love, to good works, to holiness, and to faithfulness. One of the best ways to see how this worked in practice is to investigate the many New Testament usages of the phrase, "one another." At least sixty times the phrase appears, and while we don't have space to look at all of them, I want to show you a smattering of them, several from the second half of Romans and a few more from Ephesians.

Romans 12:10 says, "*Be kindly affectionate to one another with brotherly love, in honor giving preference to one another.*" In other words, figure out how to honor one another with genuine affection. Six verses later the apostle writes, "*Be of the same mind toward one another. Do not set your mind on high things, but associate with the humble. Do not be wise in your own opinion.*" That is, learn to cultivate real camaraderie with everyone from every class; don't take the attitude, "I have my own special group, and that's enough for me. They're just like I am, they think exactly like I do, and I'll stick with them." Paul says, "No, God wants you to mingle with all strata of believing Christians."

Romans 13:8 says, "*Owe no one anything except to love one another, for he who loves another has fulfilled the law.*" You can never love too much! The bar is set too high; Christ loved us with an everlasting love. Since He poured out His life on the Cross for us, we should also love one another.

---

2. See Endnotes, page 250.

Romans 14:19 says, "*Therefore let us pursue the things which make for peace and the things by which one may edify another.*" Here Paul tells us that when we get together with other Christians, we ought to think of ways to improve their lives. We should be saying, "How can I edify you, rather than tear you down? How can I build you up?"

Romans 15:5-6 says, "*Now may the God of patience and comfort grant you to be like-minded toward one another, according to Christ Jesus, that you may with one mind and one mouth glorify the God and Father of our Lord Jesus Christ.*" That is, "When you get together, you ought to agree on life's most important activity, which is glorifying God." We should all agree on that! In the following verse the apostle writes, "*Therefore receive one another, just as Christ also received us, to the glory of God.*" Tear down the walls, drain your moats, remove the land mines; whatever keeps you distant from another person, get rid of it. Build bridges, not walls, in your relationships.

Romans 15:14 gives us one of the most important New Testament usages of the phrase "one another." Paul writes, "*Now I myself am confident concerning you, my brethren, that you also are full of goodness, filled with all knowledge, able also to admonish one another.*" That word translated "admonish" appears only here in the New Testament. The Greek term *noutheteo* means "to admonish, to warn, to teach"—and that is the best New Testament description of what we would call "counseling." In other words, Paul is saying, "When you get together as the Body of Christ, you have all of the gifts necessary to move forward productively in the Christian life. You don't have to go outside the church to get counseling; you can counsel one another. You have all you need right here."

Romans 16:16 says, "*Greet one another with a holy kiss.*" That is, extend an outward, visible sign of your genuine affection. This instruction appears five times in the New Testament. We all need a holy handshake or a holy hug—some outward, visible sign of genuine affection. And you don't get that through the TV or radio.

In Ephesians 4:1-2, Paul writes, "*I, therefore, the prisoner of the Lord, beseech you to walk worthy of the calling with which you were called, with all lowliness and gentleness, with longsuffering, bearing with one another in love.*" In other words, learn to be an eraser around people. Be willing to erase their faults. Instead of keeping a record of wrongs, just say, "Forget it. I forgive you, just as Christ forgave me."

In verse 25 the apostle says, "*Therefore, putting away lying, 'Let each one of you speak truth with his neighbor, for we are members of one another.'*" We're all on the same page; we're all on the same team. We win together and we lose together. Seven verses later, Paul adds, "*And be kind to one another, tenderhearted, forgiving one another, even as God in Christ forgave you.*" So be kind, be thoughtful. Add a spoonful of honey to your speech instead of a cup of vinegar.

In Ephesians 5:19 the apostle instructs us to speak "*to one another in psalms and hymns and spiritual songs, singing and making melody in your heart to the Lord.*" The Lord wants to hear joyful words coming out of our mouths and happy melodies bubbling out of our hearts. There's something about getting together with one another and reading Scripture or singing a favorite hymn or chorus that can be tremondously uplifting.

Finally, in verse 21 Paul writes, "*Submitting to one another in the fear of God.*" Christian men, in particular, need to remember this verse, because most of us have only memorized verse 22: "*Wives, submit to your own husbands.*" Paul has in mind a mutual submission, love, and consideration. He calls us to empty ourselves of pride and, most importantly, to learn self-control.

When the early church met for fellowship, all of these "one anothers" helped define what kind of "fellowship" they were to have and enjoy. Honestly, doesn't that sound like a great church to be a part of? If we really practiced all of these things, we'd create the best place to hang out *anywhere*!

When the apostles' doctrine and the fellowship become a priority, the natural result is an environment of love and acceptance and nurture. People can't wait to get together again. They just can't get enough of it because it's so satisfying. That's the result of real fellowship or *koinonia*.

Why Do We Need the Fellowship?

Now that we have a better idea about the substance of fellowship, let's examine why the early church placed such a high priority on it. Why did its members "devote" themselves to it? What made it so important that they placed it second on their list of priorities?

To answer these questions, let's return to Acts 2, just before the 3,000 new believers came to faith in Jesus. When some people heard the apostles speaking in other tongues in Jerusalem, they began mocking and said, *"They are full of new wine"* (Acts 2:13). Empowered by the Spirit, the apostles preached the gospel. They engaged in a spiritual activity, praising God in languages unfamiliar to them and preaching about Christ. The unbelieving world—at this point, Jews visiting Jerusalem—saw what was happening and said, "Boys, you're drunk!" Their words reveal the alienation already present between the Christian community and the city's Jewish community.

Two chapters later, we read that official persecution breaks out in Jerusalem; by chapter 8, thousands of Christians are forced to leave Jerusalem and scatter to the four winds. The door of social interaction and acceptance and love between the outside world and the Church was quickly closing. The Church felt isolated by the hostility of the unbelieving world. Most of the believers who lived in Jerusalem lost their jobs because at that time most jobs in Jerusalem had some connection to the Temple. So they had no social life or economic life, and as the outside world closed the door of social interaction and acceptance, the church began to open its own door of fellowship.

We live in a world that is never going to *really* love us, even if we live the way we should. The Bible promises, "*All who desire to live godly in Christ Jesus will suffer persecution*" (2 Timothy 3:12). If you live so nobody knows you're a Christian—if you live just like the world—then nobody cares and you won't get persecuted. But if you live in a way that brings praise to God, then you'll be persecuted. It's a given. As that persecution takes place—as you begin to feel the alienation and isolation—the only place left for you is with other believers. *That* door of fellowship is open. And that's why the church will never become an outdated institution, even in a culture as mobile and technologically wired as this one.

We tend to think that advancements in technology are going to help us get to know each other better. "Hey," we say, "now we can instant message each other from the bottom of the swimming pool!" Yet research shows exactly the opposite effect. The more technology we use, the greater our sense of alienation and isolation. More than anything, we need human touch—and you can't go to the computer store and buy Fellowship 7.1. There's no such thing, and even if there were, it wouldn't work. No computer program or mobile gadget can ever take the place of genuine *koinonia*. Adding Acceptance 3.2 to your network simply won't work.

I agree with an old Jewish proverb: "A friendless man is like a left hand bereft of the right." I might even rewrite that proverb to say, "An out-of-fellowship Christian is like a left hand bereft of the right."

With great perceptiveness, insight, and truth, Solomon wrote in Proverbs 18:1, *"A man who isolates himself seeks his own desire; he rages against all wise judgment."* As I mentally scan the pages of world history, I believe that one person, more than any other, embodies that proverb: Adolf Hitler. It was reported that Hitler despised friendships; he wouldn't tolerate them. He rebelled against any form of engaging friendships and so isolated himself.

Christian researcher and sociologist Dr. Donald M. Joy has written many books on relationships. In one of his books, he compares a person's spiritual and mental health to a four-sided trampoline, in which each side of the trampoline represents different levels of relationships. One side consists of close family, such as a spouse, children, and parents; a second side consists of other relatives, such as cousins, grandparents, aunts, and uncles; the third side consists of friends, the lifelong collection of friends who are active in your life; and the fourth consists of associates, whether they are from work, sports activities, or, especially, church."

Research shows that a healthy system has at least twenty people involved, four to six people dispersed on those four sides, and most of them will know each other. In a so-called neurotic system, there will be ten to twelve people, and less than a third know each other. In a psychotic system, there'd be a total of four to five people. Joy uses the trampoline model to demonstrate how the more isolated a person is, the less support he has, which leads to a breakdown in that person's health and well-being. According to Joy, the image of the relational trampoline shows "what everything else says about how to stay healthy: humans tend to sicken and die if they do not have significant contact even touch from other people." Joy's main point: humans are created for relationships. He states, "The base line on which all cultures and all sciences agree is this: people need people to become and remain healthy and truly human."[3]

While I would love to be able to say that the broken-down support systems describe the world, not the church, I have to tell you that I know a lot of Christians who get together every week and are *still* isolated. They're angry over this and they haven't forgiven that; they won't get together with this person and they hold a grudge against that person—and, worst of all, some of them are married to each other.

Several years ago at a Sunday service, rather than asking our people to turn around and say hello to those around them, I said, "Turn around and hug the person you're sitting next to." Later that week I received an anonymous letter. "Dear Skip," it said, "my husband did as you suggested and hugged the person next to him (that would be me). We sleep in the same bed, and until this morning, we have had no physical contact in three months."

You can't get genuine *koinonia* from a radio, a TV, or an unresponsive spouse. That's why it's so crucial to have fellowship at church. And that's why the early church considered "the fellowship" its second highest priority.

How Did They Fellowship?

So what's the best way to go about having "fellowship"? How can we effectively "do" fellowship? Acts 2:44-46 says:

> *Now all* [in Greek, this term means "all"] *who believed were together, and had all things in*

3. See Endnotes, page 250.

> *common, and sold their possessions and goods, and divided them among all, as anyone had need. So continuing daily with one accord in the temple, and breaking bread from house to house, they ate their food with gladness and simplicity of heart.*

This passage lays out a two-fold structure in the early church: the large group setting in the Temple and the small group setting in various private homes. In those days, there was a long-standing tradition that residents of Jerusalem would open their homes to visitors who came to celebrate the three major feasts: Passover, Pentecost, and Tabernacles. Willing hosts would say, "Come on in. Who are you and where do you come from? Allow us to feed you." They gave of their resources and rooms to anybody who had need.

Jews who placed their faith in Christ, however, soon found the normal doors of social love and acceptance being closed. At the same time, the door of fellowship among Christians was opening wide. So what did the new Christians do? They gathered at the usual place, the Temple, because its acres of stone courts could accommodate many thousands of worshipers.

The temple courts featured an interesting place called Solomon's Porch. Jesus had taught there. It had a covered portico area, so even if it rained, you could get under the portico and keep dry. Groups often gathered there for singing and for Bible teaching. After Pentecost, Peter also taught at Solomon's Porch, trying to explain how Jesus Christ had fulfilled the Old Testament. New believers in Christ met for Bible study and worship at the Temple; afterwards they met in smaller groups, going house to house to enjoy the fellowship of friendship, partnership, and close interaction.

In light of this little background, let's consider two important facts. First, the church in Jerusalem was *huge*. It began with 120 members, but on the Day of Pentecost, it suddenly grew by another 3,000. Some Bible scholars say that the 3,000 figure included only the new male believers; in those days, they often counted only the men and left out the women and children (see Matthew 14:21). Regardless of the actual number at the beginning, every day more and more people came to faith in Jesus. Eventually "multitudes" of Christians lived in Jerusalem (see Acts 5:14). Conservative estimates place the membership of the early church in Jerusalem (after the first nine months to a year) at about 20,000 people. That's growth! And that's a *big* church!

Second, although it was large, *all* the believers enjoyed intimate fellowship. Acts 2:44 says, "*Now* all *who believed were together, and had all things in common.*" This tells me that it doesn't matter how large a church gets; you can still have intimate fellowship in that church, so long as you meet in the large group and in smaller groups. This is a great way to mix things up—from large group worship to small group gatherings.

I think it's important to recall this historical background because from time to time I hear someone say, "Oh, I can't fellowship at a megachurch. It's just too big. We need to attend a smaller church." I understand the personal need for close fellowship, so whenever I hear such a comment, I generally put my arm around the person and ask the Lord to bless him wherever he goes. But then sometimes I say, "Now, be careful. Bless you as you go to a smaller fellowship—but maybe you should pray that it never grows. Pray that wherever you go, God wouldn't pour out His blessing upon it."

When the person looks at me as though I've gone crazy, I say, "*Every* church in the New Testament grew, if it was healthy. The Bible says, 'The Lord added daily to those who were being saved.' So pray that your new church never grows, because if it grows, then you're going to get mad again. Soon you're not going to feel comfortable with the larger size of the church, so you're going to repeat this endless cycle of moving from place to place. You'll become a wanderer because you want intimate fellowship."

The truth, of course, is that you can have intimate fellowship in either a large church or a small church. The Bible says, "*A man who has friends must himself be friendly*" (Proverbs 18:24). *That's* the key, regardless of the size of a church.

When the early church devoted itself to the fellowship, it solved a lot of problems. It solved the problem of isolation; it solved the problem of loneliness; it solved the problem of having a family, because every believer had a spiritual family; it solved the problem of meeting needs, because everybody gave of their resources to help others; and it solved the problem of instruction, because the new fellowship was based upon the apostles' doctrine.

How Often Did They Fellowship?

Did the early church meet once a week on Sunday? Did it meet every day? Or did it meet whenever a full moon came around? Acts 2:46 reports:

> *So continuing daily with one accord in the temple, and breaking bread from house to house, they ate their food with gladness and simplicity of heart.*

Now, don't worry, I'm not going to say, "Unless you go to church every day, you're not spiritual." That's simply not true. The early church had to meet that often at first because it provided for its members their only social interaction, their only family. Also, the church was just beginning, and they needed that much time together to make it all work.

As the years rolled on, however, the whole church didn't meet as frequently as it had in the beginning. Acts 20 reports, "*On the first day of the week, when the disciples came together to break bread, . . .*" (v. 7). By that time, the church was meeting regularly just once a week. We find the same practice taking place in Corinth. Paul wrote, "*Now concerning the collection for the saints, as I have given orders to the churches of Galatia, so you must do also: On the first day of the week let each one of you lay something aside, storing up as he may prosper.*" (1 Corinthians 16:1-2)

So how often is fellowship necessary? Maybe not every day, but certainly it should be more frequent than infrequent. Surely it ought to be more regular than irregular—at least once a week. Without the fellowship of the saints, I consider a week wasted. I'll even go a step further: To fail to participate in the life of the local church is to disobey a direct command of Scripture.

"Wait a minute!" someone says. "Can't I worship God anywhere?"

Sure, you can.

"I mean, technically, does it really matter that I go to church?"

Believe me, I have been asked this question more than once! But I have to say that if you need to ask the question, then something is wrong.

Sometimes a person will bring up John 4, where Jesus said to the woman at Samaria, "*The hour is coming when you will neither on this mountain, nor in Jerusalem, worship the Father...the true worshipers will worship the Father in spirit and truth*" (vv. 21, 23).

"So, can't we worship God anywhere?" You bet you can. You can worship God in the mountains; He's there. You can worship God in your living room; He's there. You can worship God on the back porch while smelling flowers; He's there, too. You can worship God under the stars, on the beach, in the mall, in your car, under a bridge, in a cave, in an airport lavatory, and even in a landfill. God is everywhere and can be worshiped everywhere, at all times, by all people. So yes, you can worship God anywhere.

There is one particular building, however, where God promises to meet with His people in a very special way. Would you like to know what it is and where you can find it? The Book of Ephesians gives us a glimpse of this magnificent building:

> *Now, therefore, you* [plural] *are no longer strangers and foreigners, but fellow citizens with the saints and members of the household of God, having been built on the foundation of the apostles and prophets, Jesus Christ Himself being the chief cornerstone, in whom the whole building, being fitted together, grows into a holy temple in the Lord, in whom you also are being built together for a dwelling place of God in the Spirit.* Ephesians 2:19-22

The apostle is speaking here of Christians, not individually, but collectively as the Church. *That's* the special "building" where God loves to meet with His people.

"Now, wait a minute," someone else says. "There's a great verse that says, '*Do you not know that your body* [singular] *is the temple of the Holy Spirit?*' (1 Corinthians 6:19). That means that wherever you take your body, you take along a place where you can worship God. In the mountains, at the beach, at home; you have a temple, which is your body. God lives inside of it, so you can worship anywhere."

That's true and that's great—but don't stop there! For Paul also writes that you are "*being* built *together for a dwelling place of God in the Spirit"* (Ephesians 2:22, emphasis added). The phrase "built together" means "collectively." In other words, instead of having just a bunch of individual temples running around, doing their own thing, we become God's building when we gather corporately. The visible, living assembly of redeemed saints gathered together is the "building of God" where He meets with His people in a very special way.

When we get together like this, God loves to accomplish what He almost never accomplishes when we're apart and isolated. Something dynamic occurs in church—call it accountability, call it encouragement—where God can work in a powerful way and accomplish amazing things that He simply doesn't do in our isolation.

And what kinds of things can God accomplish in the church that He doesn't normally do when we stay isolated from one another? I'll allow the most famous scriptural text on this issue to speak for itself:

> *And let us consider one another in order to stir up love and good works, not forsaking the assembling of ourselves together, as is the manner of some, but exhorting one another, and so much the more as you see the Day approaching.* Hebrews 10:24-25

Why do we meet together in the church for fellowship? When Christians are together, we stimulate one another to good works, motivate each other toward love, spur one another on to fruitfulness, and urge each other toward holiness. This kind of stimulation and affirmation is critical in your life. If you isolate yourself from it, you won't accomplish anything close to what God has designed you to achieve.

A long time ago a pastor visited someone from his church who hadn't attended services in many weeks. The absent believer was sitting in a chair in front of a fire, enjoying the warm coals on a cold day.

When he saw his pastor at the door, he invited him in but said little. The two men sat down, remaining silent for some time. Finally, the pastor reached into the fire with tongs and removed a red-hot coal, placing it by itself on the hearth. In a very short time, the coal ceased glowing and went dark. After a minute or two, the pastor reached for the tongs again and put the coal back into the fireplace. In no time it began glowing red-hot once more.

As the pair stared into the fire, the man finally broke his silence. "I'll see you in church this Sunday, pastor," he promised. That man had come to understand the principle: When you isolate yourself from other Christians, the fire soon goes out.

Don't be a "floater in Jesus' name." Devote yourself steadfastly to the fellowship.

An Amazing Report

Two thousand years ago, the Imperial Roman government looked at the Church through skeptical eyes. Its top officials worried, *Who are these people meeting together in these small groups and little assemblies? What are they about?* They feared that these Christians might turn against Rome and become anti-government.

So they sent spies into these Christian assemblies to find out what they were doing. The spies observed carefully and reported back to the government everything they witnessed.

I've always found this fascinating. If spies were sent into our assemblies today, what would they find? What would they report? The Roman historian Tertullian says that one of these Roman spies filed the following report:

These Christians are very strange people. They meet together in an empty room to worship. They do not have an image or icon. They speak of One by the name of Jesus who's absent, but whom they seem to be expecting at any time. And my, how they love Him; and my, how they love one another!

Wouldn't that be a pretty cool report for an unbelieving spy to write about *your* church? "They get together and sing to Somebody who's not there. They talk incessantly about a Person you can't see. Yet they expect Him to show up at any moment. And boy, do they love Him! And boy, do they love each other!"

That is being "devoted to the fellowship." Such devotion always has a tremendous effect, not only upon those in the fellowship, but also upon those on the outside who are watching.

CHAPTER 10

Eating
WITH THE KING

Imagine traveling back in history 3,400 years and standing with a Moabite overlooking the tents of Israel in the wilderness. The man looks down, sees the Hebrew camp surrounding a tent-like structure in the middle, and goes to check it out. He wanders through the various encampments, eventually arriving at a huge ten-foot cloth wall of something called "the tabernacle." He doesn't know what it is, so he goes to the gate and asks the gatekeeper, "May I go in and check it out?"

The gatekeeper replies, "Well, who are you? Any Israelite may enter."

The man answers, "I'm not an Israelite; I'm a Moabite."

The guard stops him and says, "Then I'm sorry; you're not allowed to enter."

The Moabite won't give up. "What would I have to do to get inside?" he asks.

"You'd have to be born an Israelite," the guard replies.

The man looks down and mutters under his breath, "Boy, I wish I had been born an Israelite." He sneaks a peek inside and notices a priest wearing unusual garments and offering sacrifices on a brass altar. Then the priest washes his hands at a laver and walks inside another little tent-like structure. The Moabite nudges the guard and says, "What's that?"

"The man you saw is a priest," he answers, "and after offering the sacrifice, he goes inside a room called the Holy Place. The room has a lampstand and also a table with bread on it, along with a little altar where he burns incense. The priest is going to trim the lamps and eat some of the bread and burn some incense, which represents our prayers to God. It's a beautiful, beautiful place."

"Wow," the Moabite replies, "I'd love to go in there as well."

"Oh, no, no, no," answers the gatekeeper. "Even I can't go in there. It's reserved for the priest, and to be a priest you have to be from a special family in the tribe of Levi. You have to be related to Aaron."

The Moabite continues to look inside and asks, "May I ask, what else is in there?"

The guard answers, "Beyond that first room, behind a veil, is a second room; it's called the Holy of Holies. It houses a special piece of furniture called the Ark of the Covenant; inside the ark is our Law and a few other items that represent our past." The guard pauses, then continues in a reverent tone of voice, "My friend, that's where God lives. God's presence dwells in a special way over the atonement lid on the Ark of the Covenant."

The Moabite's eyes grow big, and he exclaims once more, "Boy, I wish I were an Israelite! I wish I were from the tribe of Levi and the family of Aaron. I'd love to go in that room as well."

The gatekeeper smiles and says, "Sorry, but you wouldn't be able to do that either. Only the high priest can go into the Holy of Holies."

The Moabite sighs and answers, "The more you tell me, the more I wish I were an Israelite of the tribe of Levi, of the family of Aaron. I wish I were a high priest, because if that's where God really lives, as you say, then I would go there at least three times a day, if not more. I'd be there all the time to fellowship with this God."

The gatekeeper shakes his head and says, "Well, my friend, I'm afraid you couldn't do that either. Even the high priest is only allowed to enter that room once a year, and then only after elaborate cleansings and sacrifices. He's allowed to stay there only a short time—and his heart had better be right before God, or he'll die."

The Moabite casts one final, longing look into the tabernacle, hangs his head, and then walks away without any hope of ever gaining intimate access to God.

A New Kind of Access

The first Christians in Jerusalem lived in the shadow of the Temple, a building of stone that had replaced the wilderness tabernacle of skins. Distinct courtyards and walls of separation kept men in one section of the grounds, women in another section, and priests in yet another section. Nobody could gain intimate access to God—until Jesus came, died, and the veil of the Temple tore apart from top to bottom. Through faith in Jesus, the Lord gave people free access to Him.

The Communion table represents full and free access to God.

As you ponder the little story that began this chapter, can you understand why the third priority of the early church was the breaking of bread? *"And they continued steadfastly in the apostles' doctrine and fellowship,* in the breaking of bread . . ." (Acts 2:42). Taking Communion represents an amazing access to God that *no one* in Israel's long history—not Abraham, not Moses, not Samuel, not David, not Elijah, or anyone else—had ever enjoyed . . . that is, before Christ came and opened the way.

The Lord's Supper is vastly more than a mere religious rite that we practice every now and then. It reminds us of the astonishing price Jesus paid to win us free access to God, even as it points our eyes to His future return in power and great glory.

Several years ago, I had an assistant pastor who was buying a large amount of grape juice at a local supermarket for our Communion services. As he walked up to the cashier with many bottles of juice, a lady in line with several six-packs of beer turned to him and said, "Having a party, huh?"

My colleague grinned and replied, "As a matter of fact, yes. We *are* celebrating"—and then he spoke of the Lord's Supper. What an open door he had to talk about *what* we were celebrating!

Why Is It Third?

As we have discussed, the members of the early church gave themselves continually to the apostles' doctrine and to the fellowship—third on their priority list is the breaking of bread, the Lord's Supper.

Many people find the Lord's Supper a little awkward and even a bit strange. They can understand the first two: "Well, of course you have to have the Bible to pursue anything else in the Christian life. And I can see why you need to regularly get together to enjoy the kind of close, intimate togetherness you need as believers to survive in a hostile world." But when it comes to the Lord's Supper, they balk, "What's up with Communion? Why should the Lord's

Supper rank *third* on the priority list of the early church?"

It's a good question. And we should note that something of a debate exists as to the actual meaning of "the breaking of bread." Does it refer to the Last Supper, when Jesus broke the bread and distributed it to His disciples? Or is "breaking bread" merely a euphemism for sharing a meal? You know—"Hey, let's go out and break bread."

The answer is both.

A tradition developed very early in the church in which believers got together for a sacred meal. They called it the *Agape* or the "Love Feast." It's mentioned in Jude 12. After enjoying a meal together, they celebrated the Lord's Supper by having a Communion service.

When these first Christians gathered as a group, they took care to center everything around what the Bible says about God, them, and God's plan for them. Then, with such great teaching ringing in their heads, they could better enjoy intimate fellowship with one another. Part of that intimate fellowship involved the breaking of bread, both as a shared meal and as a remembrance of the Lord's Supper.

Understand that the ancient world attached a far greater significance to eating than we do. They considered it a sacred activity to eat with others. We tend to say, "Hey, let's grab a bite because it's lunchtime and I'm hungry." We say a quick prayer and scarf it all down; that's our basic approach. But not in those days! In the ancient world, to break bread with someone was to share common nourishment with them; a shared meal allowed them to enter into a unique kind of fellowship and oneness.

That's the idea behind Jesus' words to the church in Laodicea: "*Behold, I stand at the door and knock. If anyone hears My voice and opens the door, I will come in to him and dine with him, and he with Me"* (Revelation 3:20). A shared meal represents an intimate form of fellowship.

Although eating together has lost much of its significance, we still consider some shared meals to be very important. We still have wedding meals, for example. After a funeral, we often partake of a funeral meal. Fundraising events often center around a meal. Even in the business community, *Let's do lunch* can carry great significance. Something about eating a meal together with someone else still carries importance.

When the members of the early church got together, they shared a meal that culminated in a Communion service. It was a great tradition—but like anything else involving fallen human beings, it can become perverted. One key reason the Apostle Paul wrote to the Corinthians was that he had heard that their Love Feast had degenerated into a drunken free-for-all. So he wrote to them, *"It's not the Lord's Supper you're concerned about when you come together, for I am told that some of you hurry to eat your own meal without sharing it with others. As a result, some go hungry while others get drunk."* (1 Corinthians 11:20-21 NLT)

If the Lord's Supper had its origins in the ancient world and people can easily corrupt it, why continue with it at all? And why should it be third on the priority list of a healthy, modern church?

The most obvious answer is that Jesus himself commanded His followers to celebrate what we call the Lord's Supper. At His last Passover meal, He broke the bread, distributed it to His disciples, and then said to them, *"Do this in remembrance of Me"* (Luke 22:19). The early church understood the meaning and importance of Communion. They recognized that it wasn't optional.

When we take Communion, we remember that Jesus is making us one. Regardless of our background, gender, race, or socioeconomic status, everyone stands at the foot of the Cross.

The Frequency of Breaking Bread

Since Jesus instructed us to celebrate the Lord's Supper, in obedience to Him we partake of Communion. But how often are we supposed to take the Lord's Supper and break bread together?

You'll get different answers to that question.

Some churches say every day. Other churches say once a week. Still other groups prefer once a month. Some historians and theologians will point to various documents from church history that show the early Christians got together and celebrated the Lord's Supper at every meal.

I think it's safe to say that the early church practiced it once a week, at least in the Book of Acts. Luke reports, "*On the first day of the week, when the disciples came together to break bread...*" (Acts 20:7). There is also a document called the *Didache* (the Greek word for "teaching"), which circulated in the early churches to give instructions about proper church order. It's not a biblical book or a canonical document, but it does describe the practices of the early Christian communities, and in it we find prayers for the Communion service that were to be offered every week.

Personally, I'm glad that Jesus was not specific about the exact frequency. He just said, "Do it often." So whether "often" is defined as every day, every week, or every month, the important thing is that it is done frequently, on a regular basis.

The Pattern of Breaking Bread

But how did it all begin? Where did the practice of the Lord's Supper come from? The Gospel of Luke provides us with this insight:

> *Then came the Day of Unleavened Bread, when the Passover must be killed. And He* [Jesus] *sent Peter and John, saying, "Go and prepare the Passover for us, that we may eat." So they said to Him, "Where do You want us to prepare?" And He said to them, "Behold, when you have entered the city, a man will meet you carrying a pitcher of water; follow him into the house which he enters. Then you shall say to the master of the house, 'The Teacher says to you, "Where is the guest room where I may eat the Passover with My disciples?"' Then he will show you a large, furnished upper room; there make ready." So they went and found it just as He had said to them, and they prepared the Passover. When the hour had come, He sat down, and the twelve apostles with Him. Then He said to them, "With fervent desire I have desired to eat this Passover with you before I suffer; for I say to you, I will no longer eat of it until it is fulfilled in the kingdom of God." Then He took the cup, and gave thanks, and said, "Take this and divide it among yourselves; for I say to you, I will not drink of the fruit of the vine until the kingdom of God comes." And He took bread, gave thanks and broke it, and gave it to them, saying, "This is My body which is given for you; do this in remembrance of Me." Likewise He also took the cup after supper, saying, "This cup is the new covenant in My blood, which is shed for you."* Luke 22:7-20

I have to tell you, all of this came as a bit of a surprise to Jesus' twelve disciples as they sat around that table. As Jews, they were used to Passover; they had grown up with these *seder* feasts, year after year. But Jesus suddenly puts a new twist on it. He treats it as the fulfillment of the new covenant. Jeremiah had predicted it, and now Jesus says, "This is it." In His Sermon on the Mount, Jesus had said, *"Do not think that I came to destroy the Law or the Prophets. I did not come to destroy but to fulfill"* (Matthew 5:17). And now, at the *Pesach*, the Passover meal, Jesus was about to fulfill this ancient and great feast.

Every year the Jews celebrated the Passover, the memorial dinner that looked back to their deliverance from slavery. For hundreds of years they had toiled as slaves in Egypt, and the Passover meal spoke of God giving them their freedom. Jesus took that familiar meal and brought it to fulfillment by saying, "This meal now represents the new covenant, predicted by Jeremiah. It's here. It's new. It's now." Just as the Passover Supper spoke of a temporary physical deliverance from slavery, the Lord's Supper celebrates our permanent spiritual deliverance from slavery to sin.

Have you ever been to a Jewish Passover meal? If not, I encourage you to check one out, especially if that *seder* feast is done with a Christian emphasis: Jesus as the Messiah, the fulfillment of the Law and Prophets. It's a beautiful meal, pregnant with meaning at every twist—and *very* long. They didn't sit down for a twenty-minute lunch! They sat down all night and had a leisurely, beautiful meal of fellowship. I've celebrated Passover on many occasions; some of the most memorable times took place in Jerusalem itself.

At the end of every Passover meal, devout Jews say, *L'Shana Ha Ba'ah Birushalayim*—"Next year in Jerusalem." They mean, "We're going to make it there one day." By the way, if you ever visit Israel during Passover, good luck. All the hotel rooms are booked. It's a place where every Jew in the world wants to celebrate Passover at least once.

Luke's account of the meal mentions bread being broken, a cup of wine being raised, and then after supper, Jesus again takes the cup. It may help you to understand what happened if you note that the traditional Passover meal centered around four different cups of wine, given at distinct intervals.

The feast began with the host raising the first cup of wine, asking the Lord to bless the evening. Then prayers were given, and recitals of history were mentioned.

The second cup of wine was called "the cup of judgment," because they recalled the judgment in Egypt, focusing on the ten plagues. The host would then take a piece of unleavened bread, *matsah,* and dip it in bitter herbs, which speak of the ancient Hebrews' bitter bondage. Then he would offer a little pasty, sweet mixture called *haroset*, which is honey and apples. This points to the mortar with which the Hebrews served their Egyptian taskmasters for all those years.

The third cup was "the cup of redemption." That came after the meal, after the roasted lamb had been eaten. Once again, the host would take bread, the *afikomen*, the *matsah*, and break it, which is highly symbolic. This is what's happening in the gospels when Luke writes, "*He took the bread and gave thanks*" (22:19). In Greek, "gave thanks" is *eucharistesas*, from which we get "the Eucharist," another name for the Lord's Supper. Jesus held up that bread—they had seen it every year at Passover and had heard the words, *Baruch hata Adonai Elohenu. Melech ha-olam hamotsi lechem min ha-aretz,* "Blessed are you, Lord God, King of the universe, who has given us bread from the Earth"— But then Jesus did something very different. He called it the "new covenant." And He took the wine and said, "*This cup is the new covenant in My blood, which is shed for you*" (v. 20). The meal closed with the giving of a kind of toast.

For the fourth and final time, a glass of wine was raised and a psalm of praise was sung; that was called "the cup of praise." So ran the basic pattern of the Passover. The early church devoted itself to recreating, at least in part, the main elements of that night. That's where we get the Lord's Supper.

Throughout history, various churches have attached different meanings to the Lord's Supper. The Roman Catholic Church says the bread of Communion becomes the actual body of the Lord, while the wine becomes the very blood of Christ. That's called "transubstantiation." Martin Luther said, "No, the elements don't get turned into the literal body and blood of Christ; rather, the presence of Christ is somehow *with* these elements." That's called "consubstantiation."

As the years went on, people began to disagree not only with the Catholics but also with Martin Luther. Ulrich Zwingli said that the elements of the Lord's Supper are merely symbols of a greater reality. I would probably rest in this camp. Some would argue, "But wait a minute! Jesus said, 'This is My body'!" Yes, He did. But He also said, "*I am the door*" (John 10:7). I don't picture Jesus as actually being a wooden door, do you? He meant that He was the portal into fellowship with His Father.

These anthropomorphic terms speak of a greater reality. That's why I prefer to look at the bread and the wine not as the literal body and blood of Christ but as portals that enable me to see to the other side and what they represent—His amazing sacrifice.

The Purpose of Breaking Bread

Once you understand the background of the Lord's Supper, it's much easier to grasp its purpose. That purpose is actually threefold.

In the breaking of bread

...we look backwards;

...we look to the present;

...we look ahead.

Note how Paul instructs us to look *back* at the sacrifice of Christ.

> *For I received from the Lord that which I also delivered to you: that the Lord Jesus on the same night in which He was betrayed took bread; and when He had given thanks, He broke it and said, "Take, eat; this is My body which is broken for you; do this in remembrance of Me."*
> 1 Corinthians 11:23-24

I find it fascinating that Jesus did *not* tell His followers, "When I'm gone, build a monument to Me. I want a marble mausoleum. I want a big stone pillar at the place where I preached the Sermon on the Mount. I want you to remember Me by erecting lots and lots of icons." In fact, the only thing Jesus left for remembrance purposes was a meal.

Every time we take the Lord's Supper, we consciously focus our minds backward on the ultimate deliverance and sacrifice for our sins, which is Jesus' broken body and shed blood. We take Communion to look back, to remember. The world goes to bars where it drinks to forget. We Christians come to the Lord's Table where we drink to remember His sacrifice.

This is both good and necessary for us, since we live in a very self-absorbed, self-centered culture. Our culture tends to look at every experience and ask, "What's in it for me? How can it make me feel good? What will it do for me?" Unfortunately, many American believers take that same attitude into church. Communion wipes away every bit of that me-first attitude and places our focus squarely on what *He* did.

When we partake of the elements of the Lord's Supper, we take our minds off of everything else and remember, "Yes, Jesus Christ died for me."

Second, the Lord's Supper causes us to look to the present. Paul writes, "*In the same manner He also took the cup after supper, saying, 'This cup is the new covenant in My blood. This do, as often as you drink it, in remembrance of Me'*" (1 Corinthians 11:25). In other words, Jesus has established the new covenant. It's a present reality. We live in it *now*.

The Christian life should never become something merely to look back on, but something we experience in the present. Every now and then I'll speak to a Christian who seems to have lost his or her love for the Lord. Gone is that personal awe of being in love with Him. If these folks talk about their Christian life, it's always in the past: "Oh yeah, I remember the great revival of the past. I remember the Jesus Movement. I remember how good it was."

That's nice, but *get over it*. What is your life like *today*? How has God dealt with you *today*? What's your *present* reality? Because without a present reality, your past is invalid. It *has* to translate into something here and now. The Lord's Supper reminds us of the past, but it causes us to look to the present.

Have you ever seen the bumper sticker, "God is my co-pilot"? God isn't the co-pilot. You handed over the title deed of your life to Him. You gave Him the car. He's not the co-pilot; He's in charge. Communion reminds us, *He bought me with a price; I'm His—**Now**. Not just in the past, but right now.*

Third, the Lord's Supper causes us to look ahead. Paul writes, *"For as often as you eat this bread and drink this cup, you proclaim the Lord's death till He comes"* (1 Corinthians 11:26). As I take the elements, I remember that the very One who died for me and left to go Heaven also said, "I'll be back!" He's coming again, which places me in anticipation mode. I expect His soon return.

Jesus said to His twelve, *"I will not drink of this fruit of the vine from now on until that day when I drink it new with you in My Father's kingdom"* (Matthew 26:29).

Jesus will not take the elements of Communion again until the Marriage Supper of the Lamb (see Revelation 19:9). As much as He anticipates that great event, so should you and I.

May I ask, *Are you excited that the Lord Jesus could come at any moment? Do you look forward to His return?* "Well, sort of," someone says. "I mean, I guess it depends on when He comes."

A friend once told me, "I want Jesus to come back, but I sure want to get married first."

At the time I was single, and so I replied, "Why? I've never been married, but I have to believe that the Marriage Supper of the Lamb in Heaven is going to be a lot better than any great experience you could have on Earth." Let the Lord interrupt your life with His coming. He will anyway!

C.S. Lewis once wrote, "It is since Christians have largely ceased to think of the other world that they have become so ineffective in this [one]."[1] There is something about

---

1. See Endnotes, page 250.

Communion that makes us look not only backward and to the present, but also to the future. And so we say, "He's coming back!"

The Preparation for Breaking Bread

Anything you want to do well takes preparation. And the more important the task, the better your preparation should be. The same is true for the Lord's Supper. So Paul warns us:

> *Therefore whoever eats this bread or drinks this cup of the Lord in an unworthy manner will be guilty of the body and blood of the Lord. But let a man examine himself, and so let him eat of the bread and drink of the cup. For he who eats and drinks in an unworthy manner eats and drinks judgment to himself, not discerning the Lord's body. For this reason many are weak and sick among you, and many sleep. For if we would judge ourselves, we would not be judged.* 1 Corinthians 11:27-31

An old proverb from the business world says, "The one who fails to take frequent inventories will soon go bankrupt." Just so, the Communion table demands certain preparation. We come, we gather, we get ready to take the elements. It's a time when we reconcile anything that has gone askew between us and God.

Did you know that our Christian forefathers used to keep weekly journals of their relationship with God, so that when the time of Communion came, they could review their journals and confess their sins and shortcomings and ask God to give them a clean slate? They remembered what Paul wrote, "*Whoever eats this bread or drinks this cup of the Lord in an unworthy manner will be guilty of the body and blood of the Lord*" (v. 27).

The King James Version of this verse misleads some people. It says, "Whoever drinks unworthily." So some people say, "I can't take Communion! I'm unworthy as a person." Well, join the crowd! Every one of us is unworthy. In fact, this text does not ask you to be worthy enough to approach God. None of us can approach a holy God. The issue is that you take the Lord's Supper in a reverent manner.

An old Scottish theologian, John Duncan, was in a Communion service years ago at his church. As the elements were being passed out, a young lady turned her head and motioned to the elders to take the elements away because she felt unworthy. She loved the Lord, but she thought, *I'm not worthy.* John Duncan put his long, bony fingers on her shoulders and said, "Take it lassie; it's for sinners."

That's what the Lord's Supper is for. *No one* is worthy—but that's not the issue. Jesus' blood makes us worthy and urges us to take these elements in a worthy manner. We should participate in Communion in a reverent, thoughtful, and humble way.

Of course, we *can* partake of the elements in an unworthy manner. How? First, we come in an unworthy manner if we come ritualistically. If we think, *My heart's not in it, but I have to do this. Every Christian has to do it, so I guess I'll go through the motions;* that's mere ritualism. And it amounts to coming to God in an unworthy manner.

Second, if we take Communion superstitiously—"I'm really a bad person, and I sin all the time, but if I take Communion, I'll make it. I'll get into Heaven. This will give me some special kudos with God"—we come to Him in an unworthy manner.

Third, if we come sinfully, we try to approach God in an unworthy manner. If we approach God in the Lord's Supper with unconfessed bitterness or hatred or sin in our hearts, then we're trying to take it in an unworthy manner. We have to get right with God, which means stopping, pausing, and asking God for His forgiveness.

Fourth, if we come frivolously, we come in an unworthy manner. Some say, "This is a cool, fun little thing to do with my buddies. And it tastes good, doesn't it?" When we treat the Lord's Supper like that, we deflate Communion of reverence—and God does not look kindly on anyone coming frivolously to the Lord's Supper. Paul warned the Corinthians, "*For this reason many are weak and sick among you, and many sleep* [that is, they died]" (1 Corinthians 11:30). The Lord's Supper is serious business.

So how should we come to the Lord's Supper? We should come collectively, as humble children of God. By so doing, we make an important statement: "The walls are down between us. We're all sinners; we're all saved by God's grace, if we've called on His name; we're all in need of His love; we're all in need of His forgiveness." Taking the Lord's Supper in a worthy manner indicates that we are committed to fellowship, that we have dedicated ourselves to healing wounds and are not opening up old ones.

Lessons From a Bar

Have you ever thought about the similarities between a bar and a church? I suppose the church too often reflects some bad bar characteristics and too infrequently reflects some good bar characteristics. I think the following article, which I've pondered many, many times, sums it up very well. The author writes:

> *The neighborhood bar is possibly the best counterfeit there is to the fellowship Christ wants to give His church. It's an imitation, dispensing liquor instead of*

> *grace, escape rather than reality, but it is a permissive, accepting, and inclusive fellowship. It is unshockable . . . You can tell people secrets and they usually don't tell others or even want to.*
>
> *The bar flourishes not because most people are alcoholics, but because God has put into the human heart the desire to know and be known, to love and be loved, and so many seek a counterfeit at the price of a few beers.*
>
> *With all my heart I believe that Christ wants His church to be unshockable . . . a fellowship where people can come in and say, "I'm sunk!" "I'm beat!" "I've had it!" Alcoholics Anonymous has this quality. Our churches too often miss it.*[2]

We tend to come to church each Sunday, expecting one another to effervesce: "Hi, I'm a Christian! Do you see my smile? Hallelujah!" But what if you come in downtrodden? Wouldn't it be something if you could expect to hear, "How can I help you? How can I pray for you? Tell me anything, and I'll keep it in my heart and love you regardless."

That was the early church. Its members had devoted themselves to Christ's Body, the Church, in part because they frequently remembered how Jesus willingly sacrificed His physical body for their spiritual welfare. And here's the good news: If we devote ourselves to the same priorities that marked them, then we can build the same kind of dynamic church that they enjoyed.

---

2. See Endnotes, page 250.

CHAPTER 11

A Passion
FOR CORPORATE PRAYER

A man prided himself on being exceedingly punctual. He had a precise routine during the workweek that he followed every morning of his life.

The man's alarm went off at 6:30 a.m., he got up, showered, ate a little breakfast, brushed his teeth by 7 a.m., grabbed his briefcase, ran out the door, got in his car, drove to the ferry landing where he parked, walked onto the ferry, rode it to the business district, walked off the ferry and into his building, took the elevator to the seventeenth floor, hung his coat on the rack, set his briefcase on the desk, and sat in his chair at 8 a.m. sharp. Not 8:01, not 7:59, but 8 a.m. sharp, every morning. His routine worked perfectly for eight years.

But one morning his alarm went off fifteen minutes late. When he saw the time, he panicked. He jumped out of bed, had a quick bite to eat, shaved in a hurry, took a quick shower, ran to the car, drove furiously to the ferry landing, hopped out of his car—and saw the boat a few feet from the dock. *I can do it,* he thought, *I think I can make it.* And so he ran down the landing at full speed and jumped off—miraculously landing on the deck. After he picked himself up, quite proud of his accomplishment, the captain approached him and said, "Wow, that was a great leap! But if you had waited just another minute, the boat would've been at the dock."

You see, the boat wasn't leaving; it was still coming in.

Are you a creature of routine? We all live by routine, although maybe not to the extent of this man. We all have our weekday routines and our weekend routines. They help us manage the way we live.

The early church had four wonderful routines to which its members devoted themselves. We've already considered the first three—the apostles' doctrine, the fellowship, and the Lord's Supper—and in this chapter we want to investigate the fourth priority: prayer.

We're Praying for You

Many times I've had the privilege of attending the National Prayer Breakfast in Washington, DC. It's a wonderful event. The president of the United States usually attends, along with members of both houses of Congress and many other dignitaries from around the world.

Several years ago I sat next to Imelda Marcos, the woman with the reputation for her closets brimming with shoes. I confess I did look down to see what she had on. At the most recent prayer breakfast I attended under President George W. Bush, we heard Sergeant Douglas Norman of the Third U.S. Infantry Regiment in Afghanistan read Psalm 91 about our Lord as our refuge. He survived an attack on his Humvee that killed two of his buddies. At one point he turned toward the president and said, "Mr. President, it gives us great confidence to know that you pray, and be assured that we are praying for you."

A bit later the president himself offered a few remarks. He turned toward the soldier and said, "Sergeant Norman, your prayers *work*." And then he addressed the rest of us: "I hope America is never too proud to pray." He quoted several other U.S. presidents and reiterated how important it is that we devote ourselves to prayer—not just on that day for National Prayer, but every day.

Most of us get a little uneasy when we think about prayer, don't we? We've read the press on prayer. We've heard some of the famous quotes about it . . . and they don't necessarily boost our spirits. Maybe we ponder the famous quote from Martin Luther: "I have so much to do today; I must spend the first three hours in prayer." Or we remember John Wesley who said he had a low view of any Christian who prayed less than four hours a day. When we hear of these things, we feel burdened and bogged down. We think, *Man, if he had a low view of anybody who wouldn't spend four hours a day in prayer, then he's not going to like me at all.*"

At the same time, most of us would probably admit that we'd like to do better in prayer. In fact, we want to excel in prayer.

When the gospel first went to Africa, missionaries taught new converts to be zealous in prayer. They suggested the new believers find a spot in the jungle where they could retreat every morning for devotions. When the new believers did so, they created distinct paths into the jungle that marked where they had gone to be alone with God. Observers could always tell if someone had slacked off because the grass would start to grow back on the pathway. When a church elder wanted to encourage a brother in Christ to reignite his prayer life, he would simply put his arm around the young convert and say, "Grass is growing in your path, brother."

All of us probably have at least a little grass growing in our paths. So let's take a good look at the path worn by the early church and see what we can learn from these early Christians about reigniting our own prayer lives.

In this chapter I'd like to go from general to specific. Let's first look *generally* at the prayer life of the early church and then observe some *specifics* regarding their actual prayer meetings.

Three Basics of Prayer

If we were to ramble around the first few months of the early church's existence, we would notice three general things about its prayer life.

1. The early church prayed regularly.

The first Christians got together to find out what God wanted them to do next. They made it a regular habit. Whenever they got together, they spent at least part of their time in prayer. The events described in Acts 1:12-14 occurred just after the resurrected Jesus ascended into Heaven:

> *Then they returned to Jerusalem, from the mount called Olivet, which is near Jerusalem, a Sabbath day's journey. And when they had entered, they went up into the upper room where they were staying:*
>
> *Peter, James, John, and Andrew; Phillip and Thomas; Bartholomew and Matthew; James the son of Alphaeus and Simon the Zealot; and Judas son of James. These all continued with one accord in prayer and supplication* [strong, emotional prayer], *with the women and Mary the mother of Jesus, and with His brothers.*

Can you picture this little group? About a hundred and twenty followers of Jesus had huddled together in an upper room. Jesus had risen from the dead, which excited all of them, and then the Master had abruptly left. On the Mount of Olives He essentially told them, "Bye-bye! I'm going now, but I'll be back." And then He lifted off for Heaven. They stood around for a while, looking up into the sky, until two angels appeared and said, "Hey, He's gone. When He returns, He'll come back just like you saw Him go. So what are you still standing around here for?"

When they left the Mount of Olives, they gathered in Jerusalem as if to say, "Now what? What's next?" And so they began praying in one accord, together seeking God's direction for the future.

When we first started Calvary Chapel in Albuquerque, we began with a mid-week Bible study on Thursday nights. As it grew and continued to grow, we often heard the question, "What are you going to do now?"

"I've never done this before," I replied. "I'm twenty-six-years-old, and I don't know how to start churches."

But the question kept coming: "What's next? What are you going to do now?"

Finally, I said, "You know, I'm not sure, but let's have a prayer meeting and make that question our focus. Starting this Monday night, let's gather and ask God, '*Now* what? What's next?'"

So that's what we did. We had a mid-week Bible study on Thursday and a prayer meeting on Monday. We asked God, "What's next?"—and then we watched Him move. That's very similar to how the early church got going.

R.A. Torrey once said something interesting that I wholeheartedly endorse: "Pray for great things, expect great things, work for great things, but above all, pray."[1] Above all, pray—that's what the members of the early church did repeatedly. Luke tells us that the early Christians *"continued steadfastly . . . in prayers"* (Acts 2:42).

When they wanted to fill a vacancy among the twelve apostles (a hole left by the betrayal and suicide of Judas Iscariot), Luke says, *"They prayed and said, 'You, O Lord, who know the hearts of all, show which of these two You have chosen'"* (Acts 1:24). At Pentecost they prayed; they went up to the Temple to pray (see Acts 3:1); when they got persecuted they prayed (see Acts 4:24-31); in Acts 6 the apostles said, *"We will give ourselves continually to prayer and to the ministry of the word"* (v. 4). In fact, throughout the Book of Acts, we find the members of the early church praying regularly.

2. *The early church prayed customarily.*

In the original Greek text of Acts 2:42, Luke does not write that the early church continued steadfastly in prayer but "in *the* prayers." Luke put an article in front of the word "prayers," as if to mean these early Christians said some special prayers when they got together. Apparently they had some special method of prayer or certain types of prayers—"*the* prayers." So what kind of prayers did they pray? We can't be sure, but I think Acts 3:1 gives us a clue: *"Now Peter and John went up together to the temple at the hour of prayer, the ninth hour"*—the "ninth hour" being three o'clock in the afternoon.

The ancient Jews kept regular times of prayer: 9 a.m., noon, and 3 p.m. That's when they gathered at the Temple for prayer. At those times they said special prayers, including the *shema* and other composites of prayers from the Books

---

1. See Endnotes, page 250.

of Deuteronomy and Numbers. They often said what they called the *schmonei estrei*, which is Hebrew for "the eighteen." They recited eighteen distinct prayers; if they were very pious, they would say them at all three corporate times of prayer. These prayers stated their love for and faith in and devotion to God. Those were "the prayers."

While I don't want to imply that the early church brought lambs for sacrifice to the Temple—they understood that their Passover Lamb, Jesus, had already been sacrificed—it appears these first Christians still attended Temple services and offered up their traditional prayers (and even used this time as an opportunity for evangelism). The Temple was where the action was; that was the center of the nation's spirituality, its very heart.

If you visit Jerusalem today you will see no Temple, because the Romans destroyed it in AD 70. It has never been rebuilt. The Temple Mount where the Temple once stood still remains, however, and Israeli tour guides are fond of telling Gentile travelers, "God will listen to your prayers anywhere in the world—but here it's a local call." That was basically the thinking even back then: "Come to the Temple! It's a local call."

Remember that the early church was in transition from old covenant Judaism to new covenant Christianity. Their traditions kept them tethered for some time to their old ways of doing things, so they prayed customarily as a group at certain times in the Temple.

If you struggle with the idea that the members of the early church were still going to the Temple in a regimented way, remember that Jesus himself gave us a pattern for prayer. When His disciples asked Him to teach them to pray, Jesus didn't say, "Hey, just shoot from the lip however you feel led." Rather, He said, "When you pray, say this, 'Our Father in heaven, Hallowed be Your name, Your kingdom come . . . "

You know the prayer; we call it "the Lord's Prayer" and even today use it as a model.

Just as the early church prayed regularly and customarily, so we ought to make our own custom of prayer. My own daily custom is to get up early and have time in the Word of God and in prayer, before I do anything else. I don't like to turn on the TV first thing in the morning or read the newspaper; I figure the bad news will always be there. If I don't get it at 9 a.m., CNN will surely repeat it at 9:30 and 10:00. I have made it my custom to talk to God about my day before it gets underway. It's my way to devote the day to Him.

"But Skip," someone says, "I can't do it in the morning; I'm too tired. I'm a night person." Then make it your custom to go to God in prayer at night or at noon; or perhaps you could follow the example of the early church and go to God in the midmorning, at noon, and in the mid-afternoon. Whatever time you choose, develop a regular habit of meeting daily with God.

3. *The early church prayed instinctively.*

Whenever the church faced a crisis or an ugly turn of events, its instinct and knee-jerk reaction was always the same: "Let's talk to God."

By the time of Acts 12, persecution of Christians had grown hot and heavy. James had been beheaded, Peter had been arrested, and things were not looking good for the church. Everyone thought Peter was next in line for martyrdom. So how did the Church respond? Luke writes, "*Peter was therefore kept in prison, but constant prayer was offered to God for him by the church*" (Acts 12:5).

How did these early Christians react when they ran into a problem? What instinct kicked in when trouble arose? Did they picket? Did they say, "We have to write letters to the government in Jerusalem"? No, their first instinct was to pray.

Why is it that the first thing we *should* do—pray—is usually the last thing we *actually* do? We seem to try every other human means to solve our problems, and when nothing works, we resign ourselves to prayer: "Well, I guess there's nothing left to do but pray." Is that what prayer has become for us—a last resort? Do you know why we so often find ourselves praying about huge issues? It's because we should have prayed about them when they were small issues. Prayer keeps many little issues from becoming big. But too often we make it a last resort.

G. Campbell Morgan (1863-1945) is one of my favorite classic Christians. I find his insight into the Bible very helpful. A widow once approached him to ask, "Dr. Morgan, do you think it's all right if we bring even the little things in our lives before God in prayer?"

With his characteristic British wit, Morgan replied, "Madam, can you think of anything that's *big* to God?"

Can *you* think of anything that's big to God? It might be enormous to us, but is it big to God? If somebody says to you, "I have a cold; will you pray for me?" you'll probably say, "Sure, no problem. I have faith for that." But if someone comes to you with a case of cancer, you might say, "Perhaps we should get the elders to pray for you." Cancer may seem like a big deal to you and me, but is it any bigger to God than a cold? As the Roman centurion said to Jesus, *"Only speak a word, and my servant will be healed"* (Matthew 8:8). It's all the same to Him.

Everything that happened to the early church—small or big, surprising or expected, confusing or clear—they prayed about instinctively. They didn't have a manual on how to start a church or how to incorporate as a 501(C)(3) or how to start a singles ministry. They didn't know any of those things—so they prayed. And God directed them.

Four Ways to Pray Specifically

Would you like to eavesdrop on a wonderful pattern of prayer in the early church? You can in Acts 4, which depicts the early church's specific prayer life. Allow me to set the historical stage for you.

Another time of crisis and persecution had just begun to boil. Authorities in Jerusalem had passed a law that Christians could not preach the gospel. In fact, they were prohibited from even speaking the name of Jesus publicly. So the early church got together to talk to God about it. They gathered for prayer.

Trials *do* bring prayers, don't they? We tend to pray more when we're in trouble than when peace reigns; it's just our nature. Somebody once said, "So long as there are exams to take, there will always be prayer in public schools." I heard of a sign posted in a principal's office: "In the event of a nuclear attack, fire, or earthquake; the ban on prayer is temporarily lifted." That's just human nature.

So how did the early church respond when vicious persecution erupted against them and their new way of life? Listen as these early Christians brought their very real troubles to God:

> *"Lord, You are God, who made heaven and earth and the sea, and all that is inthem, who by the mouth of Your servant David have said:*
>
> *'Why did the nations rage, And the people plot vain things? The kings of the earth took their stand,*
>
> *And the rulers were gathered together. Against the LORD and against His Christ.'*
>
> *For truly against Your holy Servant Jesus, whom You anointed, both Herod and Pontius Pilate, with*

> *the Gentiles and the people of Israel, were gathered together to do whatever Your hand and Your purpose determined before to be done. Now, Lord, look on their threats, and grant to Your servants that with all boldness they may speak Your word, by stretching out Your hand to heal, and that signs and wonders may be done through the name of Your holy Servant Jesus."* Acts 4:24-30

In this remarkable prayer we can identify at least four specifics about the prayer life of the early church.

1. Pray with perspective.

How did these believers begin their prayer? Did they say, "Lord, we're sunk"? No, they said, "Lord, You're God." That's how they began their petition. They started by consciously calling to mind the Person to whom they were speaking. They got the right perspective and fixed it in their brains.

The phrase translated, "Lord, You are God," is a very unusual construction in the original Greek. The normal term for "Lord" is *kurios*, but that's not the word here. Instead they chose the term *despotes*, from which we get the word "despot," an autocratic ruler or ultimate authority.

We can guess why they used this term. The Jerusalem authorities had just threatened them; now they are going to take their plight to a higher authority. They don't petition Herod in Jerusalem or even Caesar in Rome; instead they take their request to the Autocratic Despot, *the* Person in Control, *the* Good Guy over Everything, *the* Ultimate Authority—that is, God.

I call this praying with the right perspective! Too often we come to prayer so overwhelmed with our troubles that we forget Who's listening to our prayers. Jeremiah reminds us of the truth: *"Ah, Lord GOD! Behold, You have made the heavens and the earth by Your great power and outstretched arm. There is nothing too hard for You"* (Jeremiah 32:17). It's much easier to pray in faith when you begin by recognizing that you're talking to *God* to bail you out, not to Uncle George or to Aunt Sally. You're speaking to God, the Creator of the universe!

During his term as president of the United States, Lyndon Johnson held a special dinner at his house for some aides. He asked one of his special assistants, a man named Bill, to open in prayer. In the middle of the prayer, President Johnson interrupted: "Speak up, Bill; I can't hear you." Bill turned toward the president and said, "With all due respect, Mr. President, I wasn't talking to you."[2]

Bill had it exactly right. When you pray, recognize to Whom you are praying.

When Peter prayed in Acts 4, he quoted a Bible verse, almost as if to say, "Lord, You knew all about this, even back when David wrote Psalm 2. You inspired him to predict the events we're now experiencing. So You're obviously knowledgeable and in total control of this situation."

If we learn our Bibles well, we'll be *great* at talking to God. The more we learn our Bibles, the more we discover His power, His magnificence, His control, His love. And that kind of knowledge prompts us to pray with tremendous faith.

I carry a little book with me called *Drawing Near.* It basically reprints, in a systematic way, all the prayers of the Bible. It helps readers in prayers of adoration, prayers of supplication, prayers of worship, and prayers of confession.

---

2. See Endnotes, page 250.

Since it has all the prayers of the Bible, it allows you to pray God's Word back to Him. I have found it a beautiful way to gain perspective.

2. *Pray with balance.*

Notice that the early church prayed with balance. In Acts 4:29 these early Christians prayed, "*Now, Lord, look on their threats, and grant to Your servants that with all boldness they may speak Your word.*"

Their prayer began five verses before this, but this is the first time they've made a request. To this point, their prayer has been all about God: "Lord, You're great. You're the Creator. You can do this; You can do that. You said this; You said that." In other words, they approached God with *balance*. They did not merely spew a bunch of requests but spent time in praise, worship, and adoration.

Too often we rush into the presence of God and so miss this beautiful balance. Our prayers frequently sound something like this: "O God, help me now or I'm *dead*! I need this and I want that. Amen." That's not a balanced prayer. Before we ask for anything, we need to stop and get our perspective, ascribing to Him worth and majesty and glory and honor.

Jesus taught us to pray this way. He didn't say, "When you pray, say, 'Our Father, *help*!'" Instead, He gave us a model prayer that begins, "Our Father in heaven, Hallowed be Your name. Your kingdom come. Your will be done on earth as it is in heaven." Only after beginning in this way did He teach us to pray, "Give us this day our daily bread."

As bedtime approached, a grandpa told his granddaughter, "Go get yourself ready for bed and say your prayers. I'll be up in a bit."

Several minutes later, when Grandpa finally got up to her room, he found her still praying. Grandpa peeked his head in the door and said, "Sweetheart, what are you doing?"

"I was just telling God that I love Him," she answered, "and He was telling me that He loves me. We were just loving each other."

The next time you have a ton of burdens you want to bring to God, how about stopping before you come into His presence to say, "I love You, Lord, and I know that You love me. Your Word says this and Your Word says that and I know You're great and awesome. What a loving God You are! Oh, and by the way, I have a few little issues that I want to discuss with You." That's a prayer with both perspective and balance.

3. *Pray with direction.*

So what request did the early church bring to God? Did these early Christians ask Him to halt the persecution? Did they request that He put the persecutors out of commission? Not exactly. *"Lord,"* they prayed, *"look on their threats, and grant to Your servants that with all boldness they may speak Your word, by stretching out Your hand to heal, and that signs and wonders may be done through the name of Your holy Servant Jesus"* (Acts 4:29-30). Notice that they didn't say, "Lord, stop their threats!" That's probably how I'd pray. Instead, they simply asked, "Lord, *notice* what they're doing."

They also asked for boldness in preaching the message of Jesus—exactly what got them into trouble in the first place. Why did they make this request? Because it was the right thing to do. And then they asked, "And please confirm our message with signs and wonders."

All of this means their prayer had *direction*. Nothing about it was vague; it was very specific. Their example shows us that we need to get away from any type of prayer like this: "Well, Lord, You know every need, both spoken and unspoken, so just bless everyone everywhere with everything." One of my professors once said, "Never speak to be understood; preach so that it's impossible to be misunderstood." In the same way, pray *specifically* so that it's impossible to be misunderstood.

What if you went into a restaurant and told the waiter, "Oh, what a general food need I have today! So please bless me." First, he'd look at you as though you were crazy; then he'd hand you a menu and say, "Sir, I need you to tell me what you want, specifically. What particular food items would you like to order today?"

God wants you to come to Him with specific requests. So rather than praying, "Lord, please meet my friend's financial need," how about saying, "Lord, Jim needs two hundred and fifty bucks this week." *That's* specific. Instead of praying, "Lord, bless Harriet," how about asking for what she really needs? If she needs a friend, then pray, "Lord, give Harriet a friend this week." Instead of praying, "Lord, bless China," how about praying, "Father, help Jesus' followers who live in Beijing to get the gospel out this week, both safely and effectively."

It's not that God needs the information. It's not as though God is sitting up in Heaven saying, "Oh, *really*? I had no idea! I wouldn't have known that little tidbit otherwise. Thanks for informing Me!" Before you pray, He already knows everything you're going to say. But He has designed prayer so that the more specific we get in our prayers, the more specifically He answers and the more effective the outcome will be. Pray with direction.

4. Pray to get results.

Do you pray merely to feel good or to get results? Most of us want our prayers to *work*. So did the early Church: "*And when they had prayed, the place where they were assembled together was shaken; and they were all filled with the Holy*

Spirit, and they spoke the word of God with boldness" (Acts 4:31).

Prayer is the slender nerve that moves the muscles of omnipotence. These early Christians prayed for boldness . . . and they got it. When they prayed with the right components, the place where they were meeting started physically shaking—almost as if God were saying, "I have heard your prayer and I have granted your request."

One Sunday in New York City, a musician put his hands on the keys of his church's huge organ—and nothing happened. Not a sound came from that enormous instrument. The custodian immediately guessed that someone had unplugged it, so he wrote a brief note to the organist, informing him that he would plug in the organ after the invocation. In his haste he wrote, "After the prayer, the power will be on."

That's the story of Acts 4: After the prayer, the power was on. These early Christians plugged into the power of Heaven through a prayer that had balance, perspective, and direction—a prayer that got results.

A Pair of Practical Suggestions

If the idea of praying as a church seems new or strange to you, then allow me to give you two simple suggestions.

1. *Learn to pray with others.*

"But I'm not really good at this," someone says. I'll bet you are! The best time of prayer I ever had was with a kid from New York City. This brand-new Christian started to pray like this: "Yo, God—it's me. You know me." I thought, *That's cool. That's fresh. That's from the heart.*

When you meet some brother or sister in the lobby or out in the community somewhere, say, "Can I pray for you?"

And then do it, right then and there. It's really as simple as that. In fact, if you want to have a lot of fun, do this with *everyone*. Just imagine your boss's reaction when you say, "Hey, how are you doing? May I pray for you?"

"*What*? Right here? Right *now*?" It would be a hoot! And it could melt some frozen hearts.

2. *Pray briefly for your country, your president, his cabinet, your state, and your church.*

Pray with others for families in your church. Don't hog all the prayer time or go off on some eloquent jag: "Oh, gracious and awesome Sovereign of the cosmos . . . " Just be yourself. Pray in short meaningful sentences, which some people call popcorn prayers.

How about coming into God's presence by saying, very simply, "I love you, Lord, and I know that You love me. I believe You when You promise this and that in Your Word. So now I'd like to talk to You about this little issue in my life . . ."

Independence Is Out

The story of the early church clearly exhibits for us the bottom line regarding the body of Christ. God created you and me to be . . .

> *interdependent* on each other;
>
> *dependent* on Him.

You won't find one word of independence in the first few chapters of Acts concerning the work of the early church. These early Christians remained interdependent on each other and dependent upon God. That's a pattern we should adopt for ourselves.

To put it another way, the body of Christ *needs* you and me. The church needs us and it needs our involvement. It does *not* need our spectatorship. It does *not* need us peering in from the bleachers or going into church periodically to get a little blessing and then go out. It needs our regular involvement and commitment to the apostles' doctrine, to the fellowship, to the breaking of bread, and to prayer.

One insightful man said, "My eight-year-old son told me a joke one morning while I was frying eggs for our family breakfast. 'Dad,' he asked me, 'how do you eat an egg without cracking the shell?' I thought about it for several moments before I finally concluded that I did not know. And so he replied, 'Have someone else crack it for you.'"

Some church people want the benefits of church without sharing any of the responsibilities. They want revival, so long as somebody else does the praying. They want good programs, so long as somebody else does the work.

But if you want some eggs, then you're going to have to break some shells. Let's break those shells together!

CHAPTER 12

Made
FOR WORSHIP

During a gathering of church leaders from various denominations, somebody rushed into the meeting room and said, "The building is on fire! We're all trapped!"

How would you respond if you had been there? It might well depend on your background, as it did in this case.

- The Methodists gathered in a corner and discussed the social and ecological significance of fire.
- The Baptists cried, "Where's the water?"
- The Quakers quietly praised God for the blessings that fire brings.
- The Lutherans posted a fire notice on the door.
- The Catholics began a bingo game to cover the damages.
- The Congregationalists shouted, "Every man for himself!"
- The fundamentalists proclaimed, "It's the vengeance of God."
- The Episcopalians formed a procession and marched in protest against fire.

- The Christian Scientists concluded there really was no such thing as fire.
- The Unitarians proclaimed the fire had no power over them.
- The Presbyterians appointed a chairperson to appoint a committee to look into the matter and submit a written report.
- And the Pentecostals said, "It's the Holy Ghost."

If you've been around church circles for any time at all, you've probably heard a number of jokes like this one. The long and short of it is that people worship in different ways, even within Christianity. Some people like it formal; some like it informal; some want it liturgical; others prefer it loose; some like pipe organs; others like electric guitars. Different people prefer different styles.

I've worshiped in many places, from stone cathedrals in Europe to dirt floors in the Sudan. And I've discovered that it's not really where you worship or how you worship, but *that* you worship in spirit and in truth.

From the Vertical to the Horizontal

Acts 2:47 provides a good springboard from which to examine the worship of the early church. Luke writes that the church was "*praising God and having favor with all the people. And the Lord added to the church daily those who were being saved.*"

That verse neatly sums up the worship of the early church. The believers were praising God (activity on the vertical plane) and having favor with all the people (activity on the horizontal plane). And what was the result? "The Lord added . . . daily those who were being saved."

In this chapter we want to consider the praise of the early church—really, the praise of the *eternal* church. Of all the activities we've been studying in the life of the church so far, only one won't end after we die. In Heaven we won't need to gather in meetings where someone tells us, "Please open your Bible to . . ." There'll be no need for that. But there is one activity that will *never* cease for all of eternity.

We'll never stop worshiping God! For age after age, time without end, we will lift our voices in joyful praise to the Lord. In fact, worship is to begin as soon as you get saved and will continue in glory forever after you die.

Designed for Praise

God designed us for praise, as an incident recorded in Acts 3:1-8 clearly demonstrates. A man lame from birth sat daily at the Temple gate named Beautiful, begging for alms. When Peter and John saw him, Peter extended his hand, lifted him up, and God instantly healed the man: "*Immediately his feet and ankle bones received strength*" (Acts 3:7).

And how did the man respond after his salvation? What was his first instinct? Praise! Luke writes, "*So he, leaping up, stood and walked and entered the temple with them—walking, leaping, and praising God*" (Acts 3:8). This guy got so jazzed that he erupted in excited worship of his Savior and Lord.

Do you know that God is on the lookout for worshipers like this? Jesus said to the woman at the well, "*The hour is coming, and now is, when the true worshipers will worship the Father in spirit and truth;* for the Father is seeking such to worship Him" (John 4:23, emphasis added).

Doesn't it stand to reason, then, that if God is looking for authentic, true worshipers, He ought to find them in His own Church? That's why the Church always has been and always must be a worshiping fellowship. Revelation 4-5 gives us a glimpse into the future, where we see the Church in Heaven. Three things pop out in this passage that continue to have real significance for us today: the priority of praise, the premise of praise, and the persons who praise.

The Priority of Praise

Heaven is an English word that comes from an older Anglo-Saxon term, *heafon*, which meant "to be uplifted" or "lifted up on high." It describes life on a whole other plane, completely different from the commonplace and mundane society in which we live.

And Heaven is the amazing spot John saw in a vision:

> *After these things I looked, and behold, a door standing open in heaven. And the first voice which I heard was like a trumpet speaking with me, saying, "Come up here, and I will show you things which must take place after this." Immediately I was in the Spirit; and behold, a throne set in heaven, and One sat on the throne. Revelation 4:1-2*

The first thing John saw in Heaven was a throne with Someone—God—sitting on it. Here's how John describes Him: "*And He who sat there was like a jasper and a sardius stone in appearance*" (v. 3). A jasper is bright and clear—almost white, something like a diamond; while a sardius stone, by contrast, is ruby red. So at the throne of God John saw a bright, iridescent white accompanied by a color like blood—as if to say we're purified and made clean by the blood of Jesus.

This reminds us that the greatest thing about Heaven isn't what we'll do there or what is there, but *Who* is there. For example, Heaven can be compared to your home. What makes your house so great? The possessions you have? No, it's *who* you have there—your family—that makes it so great. The same thing is true of Heaven. It's fantastic because God is there.

As a pastor I attend a lot of funerals. If the deceased was a golfer, somebody is bound to stand up and say, "I know that right now he's up on that eternal golf course in the sky." Not in Heaven, he isn't. Or somebody else will say, "He loved to fish, and I think right now he's up there in a boat, looking down at the biggest bass ever." No, he's not. Listen, if *God* is there, then who cares about the boat or the golf course? The best thing about Heaven is Who is there—and that's why God and His throne is the first thing John noticed when he saw Heaven.

And what kind of activity did John see going on in Heaven?

> *Around the throne were twenty-four thrones, and on the thrones I saw twenty-four elders sitting, clothed in white robes; and they had crowns of gold on their heads. And from the throne proceeded lightnings, thunderings, and voices. Seven lamps of fire were burning before the throne, which are the seven Spirits of God.*
>
> *Before the throne there was a sea of glass, like crystal. And in the midst of the throne, and around the throne, were four living creatures full of eyes in front and in back. The first living creature was like a lion, the second living creature like a calf, the third living creature had the face like a man, and the fourth living creature was like a flying eagle. The four living creatures, each having six wings, were full of eyes around and within.* Revelation 4:4-8

Come on, admit it—that's *cool*! I'll bet you've never seen anything *remotely* like it, have you? And now let me tell you a little secret (promise not to tell anybody). Before I was saved, I did some hallucinogenic drugs. I saw some wild and crazy things on those drug-induced trips—but never anything *this* cool.

In fact, nothing your mind can conjure up or that Hollywood can concoct, even with all its special effects teams, can come close to what Heaven is really like. So Paul writes, "*'Eye has not seen, nor ear heard, nor have entered into the heart of man the things which God has prepared for those who love Him.' But God has revealed them to us through His Spirit*" (1 Corinthians 2:9-10). Notice what occupies these four living creatures around the clock? Day and night they keep doing the same thing; you can't turn them off. You can't say to them, "Hey, I've *heard* that song; can we try a new one?" Day and night they proclaim, "*Holy, holy, holy, Lord God Almighty, who was and is and is to come!*" (Revelation 4:8).

John continues:

> *Whenever the living creatures give glory and honor and thanks to Him who sits on the throne, who lives forever and ever, the twenty-four elders fall down before Him who sits on the throne and worship Him who lives forever and ever, and cast their crowns before the throne, saying, "You are worthy, O Lord, to receive glory and honor and power; for You created all things, and by Your will they exist and were created."* Revelation 4:9-11

So, taking all of this activity into account—what's going on in Heaven? What kind of activity takes place up there? Answer: a whole lot of praise!

You and I were created and redeemed to worship God. The goal of all of redemptive history, from beginning to end, is worship. Did you know that? One author writes concisely, "Missions exists because worship doesn't."[1] God put us on the Earth to glorify Him; that's why He made us. We exist for His purposes, and we're here because He wanted us here to give Him glory.

In the Garden of Eden, however, Adam basically said to God, "I will *not* worship You. I'm going to do *my* thing my way, so bug off, God. I won't worship You." Self-worship is the origin of all sin.

So what did God do? He unveiled His plan for our redemption that He had crafted *"from the foundation of the world"* (Revelation 13:8). That plan called for the Lamb of God, Jesus Christ, to shed His blood for us on the Cross. Why? To rescue us from self-worship and to turn us into true worshipers.

Understand that the *only* ones who will ever be in Heaven are worshipers of God. That's what the horrifying judgments detailed in the Book of Revelation are all about; the ungodly men who refuse to worship God will be judged eternally for it. Only worshipers of God will ever make it to Heaven.

Our vocabulary gives us a big problem at exactly this point. We have trained ourselves to confine worship to a once-a-week event that we call "the worship service." Such worship generally happens on Sunday morning. We get together to pray, we worship, we read the Bible, and then we close with worship. Afterward, we go on our way, and "worship" is concluded for the week.

Sadly, it's even possible to attend a worship service and still not worship.

So what is true praise? What is true worship? Is it the goose bumps you get when you hear some hot song, a special

---

1. See Endnotes, page 250.

feeling you get such that if you *don't* get it, you walk away saying, "I really didn't worship today; the goose bumps didn't come"?

That's not it at all. The term "worship" basically means "to declare worth." The original English word was "worth ship," which simply means "to ascribe or declare worth." In other words, in worship we say, "You're worth it, God! You're worthy, God!" True worship is to declare or acknowledge worth. At its most basic, rudimentary level, worship is declaring worth or paying homage to a superior being.

But let's go a little deeper. What is worship for believers in Christ? Allow me to give you what I take to be the biblical definition of worship. I'll give it to you in four parts.

1. Worship is a response to God.

The Bible tells us in 1 John 4:19, "*We love Him because He first loved us.*" The love, adoration, and respect we give to God comes as a response to His love. He is the Initiator; we are the responders.

2. Worship is the proper response to God.

Worship is, quite simply, the right thing to do. Paul writes, "*I beseech you therefore, brethren, by the mercies of God, that you present your bodies a living sacrifice, holy, acceptable to God, which is your reasonable service*" (Romans 12:1). I might translate that last phrase, "which is the smartest thing you could do." Some translations render it, "your spiritual act of worship."

3. Worship is the proper response to God that comes from the heart.

Genuine worship is more than saying, "Okay, I'll show up. Here's my body. Respond, respond, respond. Can I go now?" Worship is the *proper* response to God, a genuine expression of praise and thanks from the heart. This is why Paul writes that Christians are those "*who worship God in the Spirit, rejoice in Christ Jesus, and have no confidence in the flesh*" (Philippians 3:3).

4. *Worship is the proper response to God that comes from the heart, whereby we place God above everything and everyone else.*

Anything other than a heartfelt response to God that puts Him at the top of our concerns is not true worship. This echoes the first and greatest commandment: "*You shall love the LORD your God with all your heart, with all your soul, with all your strength, and with all your mind*" (Luke 10:27). God calls you to love Him with everything in you. *That* is true worship!

This means we must place God above our hobbies, above our friendships, above television shows, above sporting events, and above all other relationships. It means that we have to place God above mom, dad, and the kids. A lot of Christians refuse to do that. Yet Jesus insists, "*He who loves father or mother more than Me is not worthy of Me. And he who loves son or daughter more than Me is not worthy of Me*" (Matthew 10:37).

True worship is not an act but a lifestyle. It's an attitude of absolute, totally given- over devotion to God. That's worship—and that's the priority of Heaven.

The Premise of Praise

And what is the purpose of praise? Why does God put such a priority on worship? I see two primary reasons for praise: We worship God for who He is and we worship God for what He has done.

1. *We worship God for who He is.*

God is unique from every other being who has ever existed. In fact, that's the starting point for the four living creatures as they offer their worship to God: *"Holy, holy, holy, Lord God Almighty, who was and is and is to come!"* (Revelation 4:8).

Who is God? He is holy. He is almighty. He is eternal. And this description can fit only God; no other being has ever fit that picture. Paul was never described that way. The Virgin Mary was never described that way. Elvis was never described that way. None of these descriptions fit these people, or any other people. They uniquely fit God, and Him alone.

Let me take it a step further. Because God is unique and no one else comes close to Him, He frowns on anyone imagining that he can compete with Him. Did you know that? God will tolerate no would-be rivals.

Through Isaiah God said, *"I am the LORD, that is My name; and My glory I will not give to another, nor My praise to carved images"* (Isaiah 42:8). Through Moses He said, *"I am the LORD your God, who brought you out of the land of Egypt, out of the house of bondage. You shall have no other gods before Me"* (Exodus 20:2-3). In fact, just two verses later He warned Moses, *"I, the LORD your God, am a jealous God"* (Exodus 20:5). That disturbs some people; they read a verse like that and say, "I can't *believe* the Bible says God is a 'jealous' God. I don't understand it."

Since I'm a husband who deeply loves his wife, I do understand it. I have a jealous love for her. If I see some other guy trying to pick up on her or flirt with her, I will rightly feel very jealous.

"That's not good," someone says.

Oh, yes, it is; in fact, it's *very* good. A holy kind of jealousy should accompany the love we have for those closest to us, a jealousy that protects the relationship from those who would seek to damage it. I have no respect for any husband who's *not* jealous over his wife! So the Apostle Paul wrote of the church at Corinth, "*I am jealous for you with godly jealousy. For I have betrothed you to one husband, that I may present you as a chaste virgin to Christ*" (2 Corinthians 11:2).

God is a jealous God who created us to love Him first and foremost. He alone is worthy of our worship. And if we try to worship any other person—a saint or an angel or anything else—that's idolatry, and it *will* trigger the jealousy of God. Paul warned some Christians in Corinth who apparently were trying to worship both God and other deities, "*Do we provoke the Lord to jealousy? Are we stronger than He?*" (1 Corinthians 10:22).

Even John fell into this trap—and got rebuked for it. Twice in the Book of Revelation John tries to worship the angel who showed him these great visions. The angel doesn't say, "Oh, isn't that sweet!" Instead he barks, "Get up! Don't do that! I'm a fellow servant just like you are" (see Revelation 19:10; 22:9). The angel refused to receive John's worship. Why? Because God alone is worthy of our worship—and God is a jealous God.

God forbids us from worshiping angels, Mary, saints, pastors, movements, theologies, or ideologies. Only God deserves our worship. He stands alone—we must therefore worship God for who He is.

2. *We worship God for what He has done.*

Heaven's worshipers cry out, "*You are worthy, O Lord, to receive glory and honor and power.*" Why is He worthy?

Here's why: *"For You created all things, and by Your will they exist and were created"* (Revelation 4:11).

One chapter later, John sees God on the throne with an important scroll in His hand, sealed with seven seals. A strong angel asks, *"Who is worthy to open the scroll and to loose its seals?"* (Revelation 5:2). Nobody around can do it, for no one is found worthy to do it—so John breaks down and cries like a baby. After the tears flow for quite some time, an elder approaches John and says, *"Do not weep. Behold, the Lion of the tribe of Judah, the Root of David, has prevailed to open the scroll and to loose its seven seals"* (v. 5). This Lion—the Lamb of God, Jesus Christ—takes the scroll from God's hand and breaks the seals.

At that moment, all of Heaven responds by breaking out in exuberant worship and praise. The four living creatures and the twenty-four elders " . . . *sang a new song, saying: 'You are worthy to take the scroll, and to open its seals.'"* Why is Jesus so worthy? They answer, *"For You were slain, and have redeemed us to God by Your blood out of every tribe and tongue and people and nation"* (v. 9).

The heavenly worship service continues to swell as they all proclaim with a loud voice, *"Worthy is the Lamb who was slain to receive power and riches and wisdom, and strength and honor and glory and blessing!"* (v. 12).

Chapters 4 and 5 of Revelation hearken back to an ancient Jewish practice called "the redemption of the land." If you had a piece of land and for some reason you had to forfeit it—maybe you couldn't pay your debts—it was seized. It now belonged to somebody else. It was forever lost, unless you either got it back during the jubilee year or had somebody in your family with the money and the willingness buy it back for you. Such a person was called the *go-el*, the "kinsman redeemer." So your kinsman would go to your debtor and say, "Hey, I'll buy the land," and then give it back to you.

That's what's going on in Revelation 4-5. The title deed to the Earth is in the hand of God, and nobody around has the ability or the wherewithal to buy the Earth, which was lost in the fall. So John starts weeping convulsively: "If no one is worthy to take the scroll, we're forever doomed in sin" (see Revelation 5:4).

God created us to worship Him. After we said, "I'm out of here, God; I want to do my thing my way," God sent His only begotten Son, Jesus Christ, to redeem us. And so now we say, "I will *gladly* worship God!" As the redeemed of Christ, we cheerfully and exuberantly worship God.

This means the Cross of Jesus Christ has always been and shall always be at the very center of genuine worship. Shame on any church that wants to take the word "blood" out of its hymnology or tries to hide the Cross of Jesus so as not to offend anyone! Shame on them, because at the very center of *all* of the Church's worship is the Cross. "You were slain, and by Your blood . . ."

Decades ago in the old Soviet Union, an elderly Russian woman visited a cathedral in her home city. As she walked up front and bent over a crucifix to kiss the scarred feet of Jesus, a Russian soldier tapped her with the butt of his gun. "*Babushka* ['Grandma']," he said, "are you willing to kiss the feet of Stalin like you kiss the feet of Jesus?"

She looked at him and replied, "Yes, I am—if he gets crucified for me."

The woman kissed the feet of Jesus because He was slain for her. That was the center of her worship.

Did you know the most common word for worship in the New Testament is *proskuneo*, which literally means "to kiss toward"? It's an intimate gesture of upreach that says, "I love you; I gladly and gratefully respond." In worship, we "kiss toward" God.

The Persons Who Praise

One of my most memorable worship experiences ever took place in the city of Amsterdam at what was called Amsterdam 2000. Billy Graham had assembled 10,000 evangelists from 209 nations (most of whom had to be sponsored by Westerners who could afford to fly in these mostly poor, barefoot evangelists) to make sure they understood the gospel and how to preach it effectively.

Try to imagine hearing 10,000 voices, representing more than two hundred nations—and who knows how many languages. "That sounds confusing," you say. But it was not hard at all to pick out certain words: "hallelujah," "amen," etc. As I sat in that huge auditorium, praising God with thousands of believers from around the world, I thought of Revelation 5:11-12, where John says:

> *Then I looked, and I heard the voice of many angels around the throne, the living creatures, and the elders; and the number of them was ten thousand times ten thousand, and thousands of thousands, saying with a loud voice: "Worthy is the Lamb who was slain to receive power and riches and wisdom, and strength and honor and glory and blessing!"*

Here we find elders and living creatures and angels worshiping God. Angels we know, but what about the other two? First, who are the twenty-four elders? Although their identity has been debated, it seems clear to me that they represent the Church. Here's why.

The scene in Revelation 4-5 is very Temple-esque, even though it takes place in Heaven. In Jerusalem a couple thousand years ago, twenty-four courses (or divisions) of priests served at the Temple, with twenty-four men representing each course. Those men represented the entire nation of Israel.

In a similar manner, I believe the twenty-four elders in Revelation 4-5 represent the entire Church. First of all, the word "elder" is a Church term. Secondly, we're told they hold *"golden bowls full of incense, which are the prayers of the saints"* (Revelation 5:8), so we don't have to guess about their connection to "the saints," the Church. Not only that, but listen to the lyrics of their song: *"You are worthy to take the scroll, and to open its seals; for You were slain, and have redeemed us to God by Your blood out of every tribe and tongue and people and nation"* (Revelation 5:9). What group has been redeemed by the blood of the Lamb out of every tribe, tongue, people, and nation? That's the Church.

So these twenty-four elders represent the Church worshiping God in Heaven. They are prompted by these wild-looking creatures called *the four living creatures*. The Greek word for these creatures is *zoo-al*, which simply means "a living thing." They look wild, but they have a definite purpose. Throughout the Book of Revelation we see them doing two things: They inspire worship and they judge the world. What a combo, huh?

"Hey, living creature, what's your job?"

"Oh, I get people worshiping; then I judge all those who *aren't* worshiping."

That's their job throughout the Book of Revelation. They prompt and inspire the worship of the twenty-four elders, and then they go out from God's presence to judge the rest of the world for *not* worshiping God.

Okay, so far we've seen the twenty-four elders, the four living creatures, and thousands upon thousands of angels worshiping God. There is another group who joins in the worship:

> *And every creature which is in heaven and on the earth and under the earth and such as are in the sea, and all that are in them, I heard saying: "Blessing and honor and glory and power be to Him who sits on the throne, and to the Lamb, forever and ever!" Then the four living creatures said, "Amen!" And the twenty-four elders fell down and worshiped Him who lives forever and ever.* Revelation 5:13-14

So, who's praising? *Everyone* is. You don't see just a few people in the back of the sanctuary going, "Oh, *that's* cool." *Everyone* is praising: four living creatures, twenty-four elders, thousands of angels, sea creatures and land creatures and subterranean creatures and sky creatures—*everyone* is worshiping God in Heaven.

Which leads me to the question: Who should be worshiping *now*? It's the same answer: Everyone.

Worship is not just a few songs that we sing before a service. Worship includes the entire time we gather. When you get up on Sunday morning and put on your clothes, you are getting ready to worship. And when you gather with others and somebody opens in prayer, that's worship. And when you sing songs of worship and give tithes and offerings to the Lord, that's part of your worship. And when you read Scripture, that's a part of your worship. It's *all* a part of worship.

The musical portion of worship is not a time-filler for latecomers. "Oh, man, I've got twenty or thirty minutes to make it and still get there in time for the Bible study." God intends for all of His people to gather, so that they might spend the whole time worshiping together.

I can hear someone object, "Well, now that you brought that up, let me just say that I don't really get all that much out of the worship in my church."

But last time I checked, worship is for *God*, not you. No church should select songs so that you can say, "Wow, that was a *great* goose bump I just got." Worship is all about *Him*. And since it's an audience of One, the only legitimate question is, "Did *He* like it?"

I have participated in a variety of worship experiences, all the way from a quickie thirty-minute service to a four-hour worship service, with every conceivable type of music. And I have found that I can worship in any of them.

We don't come to worship because *we* get a charge out of it; we come because He's worth it. That's worship! He is worth it and worthy to be praised. He's God and He's worth every amount of energy that we can put into our praise and worship.

Don't Let a Cat Out-do You

Wherever I travel in the world, I like to visit churchyards and look for gravestones. As a personal habit, I spend free afternoons reading these gravestones because I find them fascinating.

In Fairford, England, I once found a monument to a cat. The cat used to wander into the church building during the worship service. The townspeople agreed that the cat spent more time in the church than any one of them did in their lifetime; thus they erected a statue to the worshiping cat in the church's graveyard. You don't want to be outdone by a cat.

We were created *for* God and redeemed *by* God. To the extent that we give Him glory, we are fulfilling the reason for which He created and redeemed us. One day we're going to be in Heaven, where only worshipers will be. We ought to be getting ready for Heaven—tuning up our voices for the big day. A true Christian is a true worshiper who praises God in spirit and in truth.

May God, through His great love and power, rescue each one of us and turn us all into true worshipers who keep the eternal priority of praise.

CHAPTER 13

Worship

As A Lifestyle

I learned how to worship in a mortuary. My church at the time was looking for a place to hold its Sunday service and the local mortuary offered its chapel for our use. We had a lot of fun setting up drums and amps and singing loudly. We used to say that for such a dead place, it really came alive on Sundays.

I came alive as well.

My experience in the mortuary helped me to discover that you can worship *anywhere*. Talk about a place with built-in distractions! Imagine coming to worship and seeing a few caskets lying around, as well as bouquets that read, "Rest in Peace" and morbid things of that nature. It's a different place to learn how to worship. But it taught me that worship could happen at the Chevron station where I worked or at home where I lived or at my school. Worship can happen anywhere and should happen continuously, as a lifestyle.

A. W. Tozer once said, "Worship is the missing jewel of the evangelical church."[1] It wasn't missing in Jerusalem and it

---

1. See Endnotes, page 250.

won't be missing in Heaven. So does it have to go missing today? I don't think so.

The Position of Worship

Does the Bible advise us to be in any particular position of worship—standing, sitting, kneeling, face on the floor, face in the sky, face in one's hands? Or does our particular bodily position not matter much? Let's revisit three texts from Revelation 4-5 that give us a clue.

> *Whenever the living creatures give glory and honor and thanks to Him who sits on the throne, who lives forever and ever, the twenty-four elders fall down before Him who sits on the throne and worship Him who lives forever and ever, and cast their crowns before the throne.* Revelation 4:9-10

> *When He* [that is, the Lamb, Jesus] *had taken the scroll, the four living creatures and the twenty-four elders fell down before the Lamb, each having a harp, and golden bowls of incense, which are the prayers of the saints.* Revelation 5:8

> *And every creature which is in heaven and on the earth and under the earth and such as are in the sea, and all that are in them, I heard saying: "Blessing and honor and glory and power be to Him who sits on the throne, and to the Lamb, forever and ever!" Then the four living creatures said, "Amen!" And the twenty-four elders fell down and worshiped Him who lives forever and ever.* Revelation 5:13-14

Three times in these passages the worshipers in Heaven fall down; they're awestruck, they're overcome with wonder, and they're so thankful for God and who He is that they demonstrate it physically. They bow down. They treat God as people in ancient times treated royalty. It was natural for a subject to bow and kiss the hand of his or her sovereign. It was a sign of respect.

The term "worship" appears sixty-six times in the New King James Version of the Old Testament. The most frequent Hebrew word rendered "worship" is the term *shachah*. This word may not sound pretty when pronounced, but it really is a beautiful term. It means "to fall prostrate" or "to bow down." The psalmist said, *"Oh come, let us worship and bow down; let us kneel before the LORD our Maker"* (Psalm 95:6). The idea is to treat God like the Royal of all royals, the King of all kings. It's natural to bow down in His presence.

The New Testament features many words for worship, including the term *proskuneo*, which means "to kiss toward." Again, the idea was to bow before the king while kissing his hand or ring. The frequent use of these two words in the Bible—*shachah* in the Old Testament and *proskuneo* in the New—implies two major lessons for us: Worship involves humility and it involves our bodies.

1. *Worship involves humility.*

A true worshiper never comes proudly to God. There's always a sense of abject humility; Jesus called it being "poor in spirit." The very activity of worship requires the absence of self-preoccupation and self-focus. God is the object of my worship. The focus is all on Him.

It's something like a young couple who have a strong and mutual romantic interest in each other. Maybe they're even engaged. Once they get past the self-centeredness of fixing themselves up in front of the mirror for a date, they stop thinking much about themselves. He's googly-eyed over her and she's starry-eyed over him. They love the warmth of each other's presence. They focus on each other, not on themselves.

Worship involves humility. One of the reasons some of us struggle with entering into worship is that, frankly, we're so used to living for ourselves and so focused on ourselves that we just can't break free of our stubborn self-preoccupation. And if we can't get out of that mode, then we can't worship, because the idea of worship revolves, not around us, but around Him. It's not about us at all! Everything centers on Him.

The archbishop of Canterbury in the 1940s, William Temple, said, "Worship is the most selfless emotion of which our nature is capable. And therefore it is the chief remedy for that self-centeredness which is our original sin and the source of all actual sin."[22]

He's right! If you want victory over yourself, then become a worshiper. If God is your master passion, then you will come humbly to Him.

I submit that the reverse is also true. If you're weak in worship, then you're weak in your relationship with God. And if you're weak in worship because you're weak in your relationship with God, then church is going to be a very boring experience for you. You will come to church assuming it's all about you; but since there's nothing about you in worship, you just can't get into it. If you come for Him, however, it's a completely different story. You don't endure it; you thoroughly enjoy it. That's the stark difference.

2. *Worship involves our bodies.*

I'll be the first to admit that, at its core, worship is an attitude of the heart. It's more about what goes on inside

---

2. See Endnotes, page 250.

than outside. Having said that, however, I also have to say that in any relationship involving physical beings (such as you and me), love must be active, not passive. It has to be demonstrated.

I've been married for many years. Can you imagine how foolish it would be if I were to say, "Sure, I hugged my wife . . . when we got married. In fact, right before the ceremony, I told her that I loved her. I haven't told her since, but I don't need to. She knows I'm a man of my word. If I told her once, then it's good enough. My word is my bond."

"Have you ever hugged her or kissed her since then?" someone asks.

"Why would I need to?" I respond. "It's a matter of the heart."

No, it's not—at least, not solely. It's a matter of the heart that goes *beyond* the heart. You show it and you demonstrate it. That is why we see these worshipers in Heaven demonstrating their love and devotion unashamedly and unreservedly by bowing down before God in humility.

Of course, bowing down is only one of the physical positions of worship described in the Bible. If you were to read through the Scriptures, you'd see several other common positions that also accompany worship.

Sometimes it's kneeling. Remember Psalm 95:6? *"Oh come, let us worship and bow down; let us* kneel *before the LORD our Maker"* (emphasis added). Did you grow up in a church where you had to kneel on those horribly hard wooden kneelers? I can relate to that; I grew up in just that kind of environment. So it wouldn't surprise me to know that when you hear the word "kneeling," you think, *Oh, that's too formal.* But kneeling *is* biblically appropriate.

Solomon dedicated the Temple and worshiped toward Heaven while on his knees. Daniel faced Jerusalem three times a day and worshiped on his knees. In the Book of Acts, four times we see the members of the church on their knees in prayer and worship to God. So kneeling is an appropriate physical position in worship.

Here's a third: raising hands. Probably you've seen this position in action more than the first two we've considered. Paul wrote to young Timothy, "*Therefore I desire that the men pray everywhere, lifting up holy hands, without wrath and doubting*" (1 Timothy 2:8).

I admit that when I first watched Christians raise their hands in church, I thought they were weird. I was like that Pharisee: *God, I thank you that I'm not like these others. I don't need to draw attention to myself.* Then I discovered that the raising of one's hands toward God in worship can be very significant.

First, it denotes, "I want to receive something from God." In Psalm 28 David wrote, "*Hear the voice of my supplications when I cry to You, when I lift up my hands toward Your holy sanctuary*" (v. 2). The idea is that he wants to receive. Do you come to God expecting to receive? When my son Nathan was small, he always approached me with arms outstretched and hands wide open whenever I had a present for him. He meant, "Come on, Dad, bring it on. I'm ready for it. I'm receiving."

Second, the Bible says we raise our hands because we're giving to the Lord. In Psalm 141:2 David writes, "*Let my prayer be set before You as incense, the lifting up of my hands as the evening sacrifice.*" Just as the smoke of the animal sacrifice would rise to God and the incense would ascend to the nostrils of the Father, so the worshiper's hands went up into the air as if to say, "We're giving You now the sacrifice of our praise."

Third, raising your hands denotes surrender. Jeremiah watched as Babylonian invaders burned the city of Jerusalem to ashes. From a safe distance he wrote a little book called Lamentations in which he said, "*Let us lift our hearts and hands to God in heaven. We have transgressed and rebelled*" (Lamentations 3:41-42). Isn't this interesting? Jeremiah encourages his surviving countrymen to raise their hands because they had rebelled against God. The gesture means, "I surrender." It's almost a universal sign of surrender: "Come out with your hands up." When your hands are up, you can't do anything else. You're unguarded and out in the open.

I think it's safe to say that when the Bible talks about the lifting of hands in worship, it has one of these three actions in mind: giving, receiving, or surrendering.

The Bible mentions other forms of physical worship too. You're probably familiar with this one: clapping. "*Oh, clap your hands, all you peoples! Shout to God with the voice of triumph!*" (Psalm 47:1). It is wonderful to see an authentic, enthusiastic group of Christians joyfully clapping to their Father in Heaven.

Here's another one: standing. "*Behold, bless the LORD, all you servants of the LORD, who by night stand in the house of the LORD!*" (Psalm 134:1). Just as bowing is appropriate when a dignitary enters the room, so is standing. At a prayer breakfast I attended in Washington, DC, we all immediately stood to our feet when the president of the United States walked into the room. That was appropriate. It's the same when a judge enters the courtroom; the bailiff says, "All rise." It's a sign of respect.

I know, of course, that in many churches people have few opportunities to physically demonstrate their worship, except for one option: sitting. Everyone knows the largely unspoken rule: "Here you worship while sitting down. You're not allowed to stand or raise your hands; that's too crazy. You're not allowed to kneel; that's too formal. You are only to sit."

The biggest problem with this is that it's not biblical. I'm all for doing everything decently and in order. I'm all for unity. I'm all for refusing to draw attention to yourself so you don't forfeit your reward in Heaven. But frankly, we have no right to tell God we have a better idea of what constitutes acceptable worship than He does.

Paul put it this way: *"I beseech you therefore, brethren, by the mercies of God, that you present your bodies a living sacrifice, holy, acceptable to God, which is your reasonable service"* (Romans 12:1). Worship involves a physical demonstration of our devotion to God. It ought to engage our whole being.

The Possessions of Worship

Music has always had a profound influence on every culture. From folk songs to the national anthem, music has a crucial role to play in society. If you want to sell something, then you should probably hire somebody to write a catchy little tune and then play it over and over again. People will remember it and they'll sing it.

I still sing crazy advertising songs from the '70s and '80s. I can't get them out my mind—and I've been trying for thirty years. In fact, isn't that a song? "I can't get you out of my mind." See, it's all there. It's trapped! Songs exert a powerful influence on us. So it's no wonder that music and song is an integral part of the worship experience, even in Heaven:

Now when He had taken the scroll, the four living creatures and the twenty-four elders fell down before the Lamb, each having a harp, and golden bowls full of incense, which are the prayers of the saints. (Revelation 5:8)

The harp mentioned here is a lyre (and I don't mean a person who tells fibs). A lyre was a trapezoidal-shaped instrument with strings on it; it's like a harp, only smaller. The musician would pluck the strings with a plectrum or with his fingers and so would provide an accompaniment to the song. Here, their prayers became songs, backed up by instrumental music.

Worship involves melody and music. The Hebrew culture had *lots* of music. When the Israelites crossed the Red Sea after God drowned Pharaoh's armies, they danced and brought out timbrels and other instruments, and they sang at the top of their lungs. In the Temple they had instrumentation and music, as they did at the major feasts. Sometimes they even employed music during wartime. King Jehoshaphat had his musicians lead the way into battle—some might think he did this because he didn't like the worship group and wanted them killed first, but I really doubt it. I think the idea was, "We're going to conquer through worship and praise." And they did! (See 2 Chronicles 20:20-21.)

When King David prepared to bring the Ark of the Covenant to its rightful place in Jerusalem, he *"spoke to the leaders of the Levites to appoint their brethren to be the singers accompanied by instruments of music, stringed instruments, harps, and cymbals, and by raising the voice with resounding joy"* (1 Chronicles 15:16).

Ten chapters later, we read how David organized Israel's national worship: *"David and the captains of the army separated for the service some . . . who should prophesy with harps, stringed instruments, and cymbals. And the number of the skilled men performing their service was . . . two hundred and eighty-eight*" (1 Chronicles 25:1, 7). That's a *big* worship team! Those were the paid professionals, the instrumentalists of the nation, who led in worship. Almost three hundred of them!

The New Testament doesn't give us nearly so much detail about the musical aspect of the early church's worship. About the most we get is this: "*Speaking to one another in psalms and hymns and spiritual songs, singing and making melody in your heart to the Lord*" (Ephesians 5:19).

Do you ever wonder what the music of the early church sounded like? Don't you wish you had a CD?

We can't fully answer the question about the early church's worship music. But I do know a couple of things. First, I know these first Christians were Jewish. I know they used to go to the Temple—and if I'm reading Scripture right, the worship they were used to hearing there and at the feasts was probably very rhythmic and very loud. Psalm 150 says, "*Praise Him with the sound of the trumpet; praise Him with the lute and harp! Praise Him with the timbrel and dance; praise Him with stringed instruments and flutes! Praise Him with loud cymbals; praise Him with clashing cymbals!*" (vv. 3-5). It sounds lively, it sounds rhythmic—it sounds like a lot of fun.

Controversy has always surrounded music in church. What's appropriate for Christian music? Plenty of folks will say, "This is a church! We don't allow *that* music in here." I've heard statements like this since I was saved, and I figure that since I still hear them, we'll probably hear them until Jesus comes back.

So what kind of music *is* appropriate? I've often heard people say, "That kind of music is of the devil; Satan is in the beat. So keep it out of the church." But do you know what

I've discovered that most people mean by this? They might as well say, "God likes the music I like. If I like it, then it must be what God likes. If I don't like it, then it must be of the devil." Such pronouncements are subjective.

So is "Christian music," whether it's rock or drums or organs or whatever, of God or of the devil? The answer is this: It just is. It depends entirely on who's using it and for what purpose. If God's using it, then it's powerful. If the devil's using it, then it's still powerful, but in a destructive way.

To say that a certain kind of music is of the devil or of God is much like saying that a knife or fire is of God or of the devil. If I were to say, "All knives are evil because they have been used to kill a lot of people," you might well reply, "True, but they've also set a lot of people free who had been bound with ropes by evil men. A knife sliced the ropes and set the captives free." Or if I were to declare, "Fire is evil because it has burned homes to the ground, causing many deaths," you might respond, "Yes, but fires have also warmed people who were in danger of freezing to death." It all depends on who's using it and for what purpose.

Martin Luther was a very strong proponent of lively song. In fact, he didn't hesitate to use such energetic music in the revival of the Reformation. He had some pretty strong convictions about it. Here's one of them: "If any man despises music, as all fanatics do, for him I have no liking; for music is a gift and grace of God, not an invention of men. . . . The devil, the originator of sorrowful anxieties and restless troubles, flees before the sound of music almost as much as before the Word of God."[3]

---

3. See Endnotes, page 251.

The Praise of Worship

Did you know some studies suggest that singing can improve your health? An article called "Sing for Your Heart" lists the benefits of singing. The article states that singing could help you live longer as it exercises the heart and lungs; singing can also increase mental alertness as it promotes a greater flow of oxygen to the brain. What's more, singing can help you stay fit as it tones muscles of your stomach and back, it can keep you looking young as it gently exercises the muscles of your face, and it can even make you feel good as it releases endorphins (and without the extra calories of chocolate!).[4]

That's a pretty good incentive to start singing, isn't it? But I didn't tell you this just so you'd say, "Thanks, Skip, for the health tip." I'm saying that God created us to sing and worship. That's part of His design—we're to be singers, to be worshipers. And so we see this in the heavenly church:

> *And they sang a new song, saying:*
>
> "*You are worthy* [remember, that's the meaning of worship, "to ascribe worth"] *to take the scroll, and to open its seals; for You* [that is, Jesus] *were slain, and have redeemed us to God by Your blood out of every tribe and tongue and people and nation, and have made us kings and priests to our God; and we shall reign on the earth. Then I looked, and I heard the voice of many angels around the throne.* Revelation 5:9-11

Note a couple of important things from this text.

First, they sang. Notice it doesn't say they sat and watched *others* sing; it says *they* sang. And that observation brings up a question: How should we sing?

---

4. See Endnotes, page 251.

Do you know the Bible says nothing about technique or tempo or rhythm or beat, but it does speak a great deal about the attitude of the heart when you sing? The Bible declares, "*Make a joyful noise*" (Psalm 66:1, KJV). We are to sing joyfully to the Lord! It's all about that inner contentment in God that bursts from within as you sing. On the other hand, Scripture says nothing like, "If you don't have a good voice, then keep quiet."

Aren't you glad? "Make a joyful noise," God says. Anybody can do that!

One Sunday after a worship service I had a great conversation with a guy who seemed very excited about church. "I love it here," he said. "You know, I don't have a good voice, but if you're right about all of this, I can sing. I'm set free!"

"Not only can you sing," I replied, "but you need to sing and you need to sing *loud.*"

Here's my thinking: If you have a bad voice, then sing really loud, because that will prompt all of the people around you who have good voices to sing louder in an attempt to drown you out. Then the whole place will be filled with beautiful anthem! That may be a little warped, but that's what I think.

A counselor at a conference once advised us, "If God has blessed you with a beautiful voice, then bless the Lord with that voice. If God has given you a bad voice, then give it back to Him." I think that's sound advice.

Second, notice *what* they sang: "They sang a new song." In other words, they sang something they'd never sung before. Nine times in the Bible we see this concept of singing a new song. Usually it comes in the imperative mood, like this: "Sing to the LORD a new song."

You have no idea how many people I run into who resist this idea. "I don't want to sing a new song," they say. "The old songs are good enough. Just give me the old hymns!" They don't want to sing *anything* new.

Now, I love the old hymns. I believe in the old hymns. In fact, I've found a depth of theology and insight in the old hymns that I just don't find in many new songs. But if we resist expressing new songs to the Lord, we're indicting ourselves.

Most of those great old hymns were created from two to four hundred years ago; that means if all we do is sing old hymns, then we are saying something bad about ourselves. We're saying that God stopped inspiring people two hundred years ago. From then until now, God hasn't been doing anything special enough with His people to inspire any great new songs.

I think every generation needs fresh expressions of their worship to the Lord. And just think about it: Two or three hundred years ago, the songs we think of as "old hymns" were contemporary. They weren't the old classics; they were edgy. Can you imagine that? Edgy hymns.

And don't forget that many of them were considered controversial. Throughout church history, many followers of Christ have looked at church music and decided, "We need to freshen things up around here—liven it up, contemporize it." One of them was Martin Luther.

Luther did something bold way back in 1524; he took some popular drinking melodies and put Christian lyrics to them. He converted some bar songs, brought their melodies into the church, and married them to Christian lyrics.

Have you ever heard the old hymn, "A Mighty Fortress Is Our God"? That's one of those songs. "Away in a Manger" is another one. Just imagine, when Martin Luther first started singing "Away in a Manger"—a bar melody the world sang—some Christians said, "He can't do that! That's of the devil. What a scandal!" Who today would think "Away in a Manger" is of the devil? It's a classic. But it wasn't back then.

Consider what Martin Luther once said: "How has it happened that in the secular field there are so many fine poems and so many beautiful songs, while in the religious field we have such rotten, lifeless stuff?"[5] Okay, Marty—tell us how you really feel! I think I would have liked Martin Luther.

In 1690, a young boy complained to his father, "Dad, the songs at church are boring." His dad got very angry with him and said, "If you think you can do better, then you ought to write your own."

So he did.

Young Isaac Watts decided, "We need some new songs." And he wrote such tunes as, "When I Survey the Wondrous Cross" and "Joy to the World!" But when he wrote them, they weren't classics.

Then there was William Booth. In 1865, William Booth decided the church music of his era needed to be updated. He was tired of the organ, so he decided *I'm going to bring in trumpets; that's what the Bible says to do, right? "Praise Him with trumpets and praise Him with drums and cymbals."* He took his new music out of the church and into the streets because he felt, "Those people will never come in and hear this stuff." So he brought the new stuff to them—and when he did, church leaders said, "That's devil music!" But we thank God for the Salvation Army and for what William Booth did.

Then there was Dwight L. Moody, who held revival meetings all over the United States and Europe. D.L.

---

5. See Endnotes, page 251.

Moody was the designated preacher, but he had a worship leader named Ira Sankey. Sankey took some contemporary songs, like Luther before him—mainly the waltzes (those were the edgy dances back then)—and brought them into the church, adding Christian lyrics to them. Imagine what would happen if we were to take an Eminem song and put worship words to it. That's what it would be like. It would be fun just to watch people's reactions!

Moody took the new music with him to Glasgow in 1874, and when Sankey sang before and after the crusades, the Scottish church said, "That's steam kettle music" (meaning it was loud and noisy). Up to that point, the Scottish church had put music only to the Psalms of David; it was critical of any new forms.

Criticism of *any* new church music has gone on for a *very* long time.

A word to you musicians out there: Would you please write us some new hymns? Would you create for us some fresh expressions? "I'd like to," you say, "but my style is a little bit different." Good! Bring it on. "But you may not be used to it," you say. *Great!* Bring it on. Let's try it out. Let's see what the Lord might wish to do with it.

Remain open to new songs and new beats and new rhythms. Be open to new songs while still loving the old songs. Sing *all kinds* of songs. You may say, "Well, I'm not going to sing a song I don't like." Okay—but you love *Him*, don't you? Then sing!

Redeemed for Worship

Let's begin to see worship as the prime activity of the Christian. God called us out of the world as non-worshipers to be transformed into worshipers. It is the prime activity of all believers in Jesus—not a once-a-week activity, but a lifestyle. We're created and redeemed for it!

Worship is a surrender. In worship we give ourselves completely over to Him and express our deep love for Him.

If you don't want to raise your hands, then don't. If you're the kind of believer who says, "I'm just not one of *those*," then don't do it. And don't worry about it. It's not as though you have to do it. If you want to do it, then do it. If you want to stand up, then stand. If there's a moment when you feel especially moved and you want to bow down, then bow. Now, remain sensitive to others. Don't do it to draw attention to yourself; make sure you direct all attention to the Lord. Because He's worth it!

An unknown author once wrote a short piece called "Visiting Day." I think it's a good reminder for us about the importance of worship as a lifestyle:

> *He had been looking forward to this moment all day long; after six days of labor it finally arrived. It's Visiting Day! The man with the keys arrives to swing open the large, heavy doors. The cold, gray hall springs to life in the warm glow of the light. He can hardly control his emotions.*
>
> *The families begin to arrive. He peers from the corner of the room, longing for the first glimpse of his loved ones. He lives for the weekends; he lives for these visits.*
>
> *As the cars arrive he watches intently. Then finally they arrive, for whom he would do anything. They embrace, they eat a light lunch and reminisce on how things used to be. At one point they break into singing, with interruptions and laughter and applause. But all too soon it's over. A tear comes to his eye as they depart. Then the man with the keys*

closes the heavy doors, and he hears the key turn in the lock, marking the end of a special day. There he stands, alone again. He knows that most of his visitors will not contact him again until next week. As the last car pulls away from the parking lot, Jesus retreats into loneliness as He waits till next Sunday, Visiting Day.

It's very sad, but a large percentage of churchgoers seem to view Sunday as Visiting Day. One observer noted that we've become a generation of people who worship our work, we work at our play, and we play at our worship.

As your car pulls away from the parking lot this Sunday, it's my sincere prayer that Jesus won't be saying, "I'll have to wait another week until Visiting Day." I pray instead that you'll walk out of the service, get in your car, and say, "It's time to worship!" And as you drive down the street a song will come into your mind and you'll worship. Or tomorrow at work you'll pause and worship the Lord in some fashion. That's when a big smile will cross Jesus' face—when worship becomes the natural, unending worship of your heart.

CHAPTER 14

You're On A Mission

FROM GOD

Do you like to fish? I'm not a great fisherman; I've never really gotten into it. My dad was *big* into it, and I suspect he was a little disappointed that I wasn't.

Although I've never gotten into fishing, one of my friends loves it. He once took me up into the Sierra Mountains and talked the whole time about the wonders of fly-fishing. "It's the greatest thing in the world!" he enthused. Later he got a little less excited after I contracted a nice case of beginner's luck and caught the biggest fish on our trip.

Since that trip I have discovered something about fishing: The best fishing holes are sometimes hard to reach. Would you rather fish in a place where thousands of people are stepping over each other to get to the fish and where the same lake has been fished with the same bait for many decades? Or would you rather visit a remote place that is difficult to reach in a more dangerous and primitive environment, yet where the fishing is really good?

It may surprise you, but I've just described missions to you.

Toward the beginning of His earthly ministry, Jesus visited some fishermen on the Sea of Galilee and said to them,

"Follow Me, and I will make you become fishers of men" (Mark 1:17). Fishing is at the heart of missions.

"Go," Not "Come"

I find it noteworthy that while Jesus never once said to a worldly crowd, "Come to church," He did say to the Church, "Go to the world."

We call His famous instruction "the Great Commission." Mark states it very succinctly: *"Go into all the world and preach the gospel to every creature. He who believes and is baptized will be saved; but he who does not believe will be condemned"* (Mark 16:15-16).

Go, not come.

Leave, not stay.

Scatter strategically, not just hang out.

Furthermore, just before He ascended into Heaven, Jesus gave His disciples the pattern for this "going." He said, *"You shall receive power when the Holy Spirit has come upon you; and you shall be witnesses to Me in Jerusalem, and in all Judea and Samaria, and to the ends of the earth"* (Acts 1:8).

Through much of this book we've camped in and around Acts 2. We've looked at what happens when the church gathers—but so far we've only briefly identified

what lies on either side of this passage.

And what's on either side is evangelism.

Acts 2:40-41 says, *"And with many other words he* [Peter] *testified and exhorted them, saying, 'Be saved from this perverse generation.' Then those who gladly received his word were baptized; and that day about three thousand souls were added to them."* Six verses later we see a pattern developing: *"And the Lord added to the church daily those who were being saved"* (Acts 2:47).

Reading through the Book of Acts, you discover the pattern of evangelism: Jesus mandated the Church to go to Jerusalem first, then Judea, Samaria, and to the uttermost parts of the world. By Acts 8, the Church is going outside of Jerusalem into Judea and Samaria, and then for the rest of the book you see its representatives launching out to the far corners of the Earth.

After Pentecost, the disciples remembered that Jesus had said to them, *"As the Father has sent Me, I also send you"* (John 20:21). He basically told them, "I'm on a mission from God—and now I'm giving you the same mission."

It would be good, I believe, if we all began to think differently about our lives. In fact, we are *all* on a mission from God. All of us who follow Christ are missionaries. To some degree, we all have a sphere of influence into which Jesus sends us as His witnesses and ambassadors.

So then—how well are you doing on your mission from God?

Evangelize or Fossilize

In the main courtyard of our church we have a sign inscribed in stone that says, "Go into all the world," signed, "Jesus Christ." We want every member of our congregation to see that message and think about it repeatedly every time they leave the grounds.

It's about His work. Remember the quote by Oswald J. Smith: "The church that does not evangelize will fossilize." That's true not only of a church but also of an individual. The Christian who does not evangelize will eventually fossilize. While we love it when men and women come to faith in Christ during a worship service, certainly a large part of a church's evangelism should take place outside of its borders, where the fishing is good and the fish are really hungry.

I have a book in my library that I bought just because of the title: *Why Churches Die*. I've always been a student of the church. At the beginning of his book, Hollis Green gives several reasons for churches dying; then he elaborates on them. So why do churches die? "Number one," Green wrote, "converts don't become disciples. And number two, disciples don't become apostles, ones who are sent out to do God's work."[1] When converts don't become disciples and disciples don't become apostles, churches die.

On the other hand, when churches actively *"Go . . . and make disciples"* (Matthew 28:19), oh, how they thrive! A healthy involvement in missions is a sign of maturity for any group of believers, maturity that leads to growth in the church.

You're on a mission from God! But why has Jesus sent you on this mission? Let me give you several reasons.

Reason One: The Character of God

Someone once said, "If you're going to follow Jesus Christ, then you must follow Him to the ends of the Earth, because that's where He's going." I've discovered something about God: He's all about sending. In fact, as I read through Scripture, I find His constant message is missions. God *sends* people.

I could begin with Abraham: *"Now the LORD had said to Abram, 'Get out of your country, from your family and from*

1. See Endnotes, page 251.

your father's house, to a land that I will show you'" (Genesis 12:1). God sent Abraham away from his homeland. And what was the purpose of his leaving? Just so he would have an adventure? Hardly! God said, "*In you all the families of the earth shall be blessed*" (Genesis 12:3). In other words, "Abraham, the purpose of this mission—the reason I'm sending you from Ur of the Chaldeans to this new land that I'm going to give your descendants—is that eventually the Messiah is going to come through your family line. And through Him, Jesus Christ, all the nations of the world will be blessed."

Blessing is the purpose of any mission organization. Through our mission, our sending, our going out, the world will be blessed through the seed of Abraham, Jesus Christ.

As the Old Testament unfolds, however, we see a tragedy taking place. As time went on, Israel largely forgot her calling to be a light to the rest of the world. Instead, the nation turned inward and became all about Israel. It became like a submarine, submerged and preoccupied with its own stuff. When it didn't turn outward, it began to go stale.

That's why God sent prophet after prophet to His people, speaking to them with words like those in Psalm 2: "*Ask of Me, and I will give You the nations for Your inheritance, and the ends of the earth for Your possession*" (v. 8). Or He spoke as He did in a passage from Isaiah: "*I will also give You as a light to the Gentiles, that You should be My salvation to the ends of the earth*" (Isaiah 49:6). God's whole Old Testament mentality focused on missions.

When we move into the New Testament, we discover Jesus Christ. Talk about a cross-cultural mission! He left Heaven and came all the way down to the Earth. Why? Because the Son was on a mission from the Father (see John 5:30).

If you've ever traveled to a foreign country, you've probably experienced some of what's often called "culture shock." You crave a McDonald's—and it's not there. The people drive a bit differently, you smell a lot of unfamiliar odors, you witness alien ways of doing things, you taste odd foods—everything seems different. You almost can't help going through a period of shock; it's just so *different* from what you're used to in the United States. So imagine the shock of leaving Heaven and coming to the Earth as Jesus did. Paul wrote that Jesus "*. . . made Himself of no reputation, taking the form of a bondservant*" (Philippians 2:7). Any missionary who has to pour himself out to adapt to a foreign culture experiences some of this (although not to the degree that Jesus did).

So we see that one of the central acts of the Father and Jesus is to send us out to the world. And what can we learn about the Holy Spirit? Well, you can hardly go anywhere in the Book of Acts without noticing that the Holy Spirit is all about missions. Sixty times in the Book of Acts, the Holy Spirit orchestrates the proclamation of the gospel as it goes out from Jerusalem to Judea and to the farthest reaches of the Earth. Sixty times He directs it and empowers it! Remember what Jesus said to His followers: "*You will be* filled with the Spirit *and be my witnesses in Jerusalem, Judea, Samaria, and to the uttermost parts of the earth*" (Acts 1:8, paraphrase, emphasis added).

Robert Speer, who led the student volunteer movement, once said, "We cannot think of God without . . . thinking of Him as a missionary God."[2] Why are you on a mission from God? You're on that mission because of the character of the God you serve.

---

2. See Endnotes, page 251.

Reason Two: The Condition of the Harvest

When Jesus started traveling from village to village and city to city, preaching the gospel and healing every kind of human disease, the plight of the Israelites that He observed moved Him deeply. "*When He saw the multitudes,*" Matthew reports, "*He was moved with compassion for them, because they were weary and scattered, like sheep having no shepherd*" (Matthew 9:36).

As Jesus considered the wretched shape of this flock, He turned to His disciples and said, "*The harvest truly is plentiful, but the laborers are few. Therefore pray the Lord of the harvest to send out laborers into His harvest*" (vv. 37-38).

Jesus saw the crowds differently than we sometimes see them. We often see crowds as a pain. We consider them obnoxious. "They're hindering where I want to go! They're crowding me! I don't like them so close!" Jesus had compassion on the multitudes because they had grown weary and scattered, which speaks of an inward condition of the soul. One translation says, "He noticed that they were exhausted by their troubles and their long, aimless wandering."[3] So Jesus looked beyond the withered arm or the blind eye or the deaf ear and noticed, most of all, their weary condition of soul. *That's* how He viewed the harvest. Jesus cared—and that's how missions always begins. It begins with a care, a deep concern. That's the bottom line.

J.C. Ryle, an English bishop from the nineteenth century, once said, "The highest form of selfishness is a man content to go to heaven alone."[4] Think about that: "The highest form of selfishness is a man content to go to Heaven alone." We can talk all day about how the church should strategize

---

3. See Endnotes, page 251.
4. See Endnotes, page 251.

and mobilize and organize missions, but it's nothing but window dressing without an essential ingredient: A genuine concern for the lost. Unless we begin to look at people differently than perhaps we have looked at them in the past, missions will stay stuck in neutral.

Jesus saw the people as weary, exhausted by their troubles—and His concern motivated Him to action. As Jesus entered Jerusalem just a few days before His crucifixion, He looked out over the city and sighed, *"O Jerusalem, Jerusalem, the one who kills the prophets and stones those who are sent to her! How often I wanted to gather your children together, as a hen gathers her chicks under her wings, but you were not willing!"* (Matthew 23:37). That's a *deep* concern.

The Apostle Paul caught this same concern from his Master. He writes, *"I have great sorrow and continual grief in my heart. For I could wish that I myself were accursed from Christ for my brethren, my countrymen according to the flesh, who are Israelites"* (Romans 9:2-4). Leading a person to Christ begins with loving a person enough to have a genuine concern for his or her soul.

Whenever a church starts turning inward and designs all of its activities to help its members enjoy one another—if it gets consumed with that—then it's on the way down. That's where the fossilization takes place. William Temple once said, "The church is the only society on earth that exists for the benefit of non-members."[5]

When Jesus said, "The harvest is truly plentiful but the laborers are few. Therefore pray the Lord of the harvest to send out laborers into His harvest," notice that He instructed His disciples to pray for workers, not supervisors. We don't need armchair quarterbacks. We don't need people to say,

---

5. See Endnotes, page 251.

"I'm looking for a career and ministry that seems cool." Jesus wants workers who will do the hard work. He wants people who are willing to be sent.

If you were to line up all of the lost people on planet Earth and place them back to back, I am told you would form a line that would circle the globe thirty times—and the line grows twenty miles longer every day. That's what we're up against!

The harvest is truly plentiful, but the laborers—the workers, the volunteers, the goers—are few. Therefore, pray the Lord of the harvest will send out workers.

Reason Three: The Commission of Jesus

Jesus said, "Go." So if the Lord says, "Go," how can we say, "But why?" If God says, "Jump," we should respond, "How high?" If the Lord says, "Go," we must say, "Where? When? How?" This is the first and foremost reason why missions is so vital: Because Jesus said, "Go into all the world."

It's interesting that just one chapter after Jesus told His disciples to "pray to the Lord of the harvest to send out laborers into the harvest field," He told the twelve—the ones He had instructed to pray—to "go." Now, think about that for a moment. Picture it in your mind.

"I want you guys to pray because the harvest is great and we need workers."

"Okay, Lord, we'll do that. 'Father, we pray that You'll send out workers into the harvest field. Amen.'"

Almost as soon as they're done, Jesus tells them, "Okay, I'm going to answer your prayer. *Go!*"

I find this to be a consistent pattern, both in the Bible and in history. As God gives us a heart for people around the world and we start praying for them, that heart gets translated into, "I want to do more." And soon *we* become the ones who go.

Now, what is the commission that Jesus gave? "Go into all the world. Begin at Jerusalem, expand into Judea and Samaria and then to the uttermost parts of the earth." Sometimes we forget this commission and give into various objections that people raise.

"Christianity is a Western religion; it's for people in the West."

Excuse me, but it started in the East, not the West!

"You have no right to impose your Christian values on people around the world."

There is little tolerance today for missions, very little sympathy for the idea of going out, leaving your culture, and talking to everyone around the world about their need for Jesus Christ. From the media to the academic world to even some churches, there is a deep criticism of going out to proclaim the gospel. The world would prefer that Christians quietly stick to acts of service like feeding the poor, healing the sick, and encouraging the brokenhearted. While all this may sound politically correct, it's clearly missing a huge aspect of spiritual correctness. We are to be salt and light in this world and to help those around us, and the best way to do that is to proclaim the ultimate message of help: Jesus came into the world to seek and save those who are lost (see Luke 19:10); He is the way, the truth, and the life and no one comes to the Father except through Him (see John 14:6).

When Jesus arrived on the scene in Bethlehem, did the angel announce the good news like this: "I bring you good tidings which shall be . . . " to a few people? To the people living right in Bethlehem? To Americans later in history? No, he said, *"I bring you good tidings of great joy which will be to* all *people"* (Luke 2:10, emphasis added). *All* men and women, everywhere. *"For God so loved the* world *that He gave His only begotten Son"* (emphasis added). John 3:16 doesn't say, "For God so loved America and the Western culture that spawned it." The gospel is for *everyone.*

Faith in Christ is the cure for the fatal disease of sin. Just as the treatment for heart disease, lung disease, or any other disease is universal—the same treatment for cancer works in India as well as it does in America—so the cure for sin is the same in England, in America, in China, in India, and in Sri Lanka, as it is anywhere else. It's the same cure: it's Jesus and His blood.

And He's the doctor who tells all of us, "Go! You have the cure. Go into all the world and bring the cure to everyone, everywhere."

Reason Four: The Return of Jesus

Jesus is coming back to Earth very soon! And we have a limited amount of time to get the news out about His universal cure for sin. Luke writes:

> *The former account I made, O Theophilus, of all that Jesus began both to do and to teach* [which implies He's not done yet; He started something], *until the day in which He was taken up, after He through the Holy Spirit had given commandments to the apostles whom He had chosen, to whom He also presented Himself alive after His suffering by many infallible proofs, being seen by them during forty days and speaking of the things pertaining to the kingdom of God. And being assembled together*

with them, He commanded them not to depart from Jerusalem, but to wait for the Promise of the Father, "which," He said, "you have heard from Me; for John truly baptized with water, but you shall be baptized with the Holy Spirit not many days from now." Therefore, when they had come together, they asked Him, saying, "Lord, will You at this time restore the kingdom to Israel?" And He said to them, "It is not for you to know times or seasons which the Father has put in His own authority. But you shall receive power when the Holy Spirit has come upon you; and you shall be witnesses to Me in Jerusalem, and in all Judea and Samaria, and to the end of the earth." Acts 1:1-8

Jesus had told His followers to wait in Jerusalem until they had received the Holy Spirit and the power He would give them to accomplish the Great Commission. He had a very definite purpose for the power—but they interrupted Him to say, "So, *now* are you going to give us back the kingdom? You know, it's all about us." The disciples had focused almost entirely on themselves.

Jesus dismissed their question with a quick, "Don't worry about that. Don't worry about setting the date; you just get busy. You shall be filled with the Holy Spirit and He will enable you to be my witnesses in Jerusalem, Judea, Samaria, and the ends of the earth."

Just after Jesus gave His followers their final marching orders, He ascended into Heaven and disappeared from their sight. Can you imagine? Wow! Luke continues:

And while they looked steadfastly toward heaven as He went up, behold, two men stood by them in white apparel, who also said, "Men of Galilee, why do you stand gazing up into heaven? This same Jesus, who

> *was taken up from you into heaven, will so come in like manner as you saw Him go into heaven."*
> Acts 1:10-11

The original Greek text translated, "They looked steadfastly toward heaven," suggests that the disciples stood there for an extended period of time, just gazing up into the sky long after Jesus had disappeared. Finally a couple of angels had to redirect their attention. In a blunt manner, as agents tend to do, they asked, "What are you doing, staring up into Heaven? You've been given a commission, boys, and you have a limited amount of time in which to fulfill that commission. He's coming again! He'll come back, just as you saw Him go."

Jesus is coming again!

Think of it this way: Whether the Lord returns next week or you die in a year, once you're in Heaven, you'll never again be able to witness to another lost person—*Ever*. The opportunity will be gone for good.

"Did you know that Jesus loves you and has a wonderful plan for your life?"

"Why, yes I did. That's why I'm here with you in Heaven."

All opportunities to introduce people to Jesus are here, on this fallen planet. You'll never be able to pass out another tract in Heaven; you'll never be able to support a missionary in Heaven; you'll never be able to go into all the world in Heaven. By then, it'll be too late. The opportunity we have between the First and Second Coming is our only opportunity to witness to the salvation available in Jesus Christ alone.

In His last recorded message in the Bible, three times Jesus repeats himself. Can you guess what that message is?

"Behold," He says, *"I am coming quickly!"* (Revelation 22:7, 12, 20). I know what you might be thinking: *Yeah, but that was written two thousand years ago. I don't think it's that quick. He hasn't come back yet!* The point is that we expect Him to come at any moment. We don't know the day or the hour; we are simply told to march ahead and be ready whenever He returns.

Paul writes, *"We should live soberly, righteously, and godly in this present age, looking for the blessed hope and glorious appearing of our great God and Savior Jesus Christ"* (Titus 2:12-13). Peter adds, *"With the Lord one day is as a thousand years, and a thousand years as one day"* (2 Peter 3:8). If you think it's been a long time since Jesus promised to return "quickly," just remember that in God's economy, it's been only two days! Less than a week ago, by Heaven's clock, Jesus said, "I am coming quickly."

Reason Five: The Coming Judgment

Go back in your mind to Matthew 9, when Jesus looked at the bedraggled crowds and had compassion on them. "[Look]," He told His disciples, *"the harvest truly is plentiful, but the laborers are few. Therefore pray the Lord of the harvest to send out laborers"* (vv. 37-38).

When we hear the word "harvest" from that passage, typically we think it implies evangelism. But if you follow the theme "harvest" through both the Old and New Testaments, you'll see that far more often the term describes judgment.

A man traveling through a country looked out of his window and saw the fields all white in color. He asked the guide with him, "Why are the fields so white? What is that?"

"Oh," he replied, "it's because the wheat is ready."

"Wheat?" the man wondered aloud. "I always thought wheat was golden."

The guide chuckled and said, "Wheat *is* golden—unless it's overripe. When that happens, it lightens up." Afterward the man wrote, "Then it dawned on me, that's why Jesus told His disciples that the fields were white—the grain had to be gleaned *immediately*. They were overripe and the judgment was coming."

When God speaks in the Bible of the harvest, usually He has in mind the coming judgment. We have a limited amount of time to declare the good news before the wicked are judged.

When God described the coming overthrow of Babylon, He said, *"Babylon is like a threshing floor when it is time to thresh her; yet a little while and the time of her harvest will come"* (Jeremiah 51:33).

Through the prophet Joel, God described the future judgment of the nations: *"Put in the sickle, for the harvest is ripe. Come, go down; for the winepress is full, the vats overflow—for their wickedness is great"* (Joel 3:13).

Jesus said plainly, *"The harvest is the end of the age, and the reapers are the angels. Therefore as the tares are gathered and burned in the fire, so it will be in the end of this age"* (Matthew 13:39-40).

Jesus had compassion on the crowds because He saw them weary and emotionally scattered. So He told His disciples, "Pray to the Lord of the harvest." Yes, He had compassion on the weariness of the people, but He had even more compassion because He knew divine judgment was coming and that they would never again have another opportunity to escape it. The harvest was coming—bringing devastating consequences.

Let's Go Fishing

I'd like to conclude with a modern-day parable. I hope it motivates you as much as it does me.

Once a group of men called themselves fishermen. There were many fish in the waters all around them; in fact, the whole area was dotted with streams and lakes brimming with fish. And those fish were hungry! Week after week, month after month, and year after year, those who called themselves fishermen met and talked about their call to fish, the abundance of fish, and how they might go about fishing. They pled that everyone should be a fisherman and every fisherman should fish. There was only one thing they never did: They did not fish.

Once they organized a board to send out fishermen to other places teeming with fish. The board hired staff and appointed committees and held many meetings to define fishing, defend fishing, and decide what new stream they should think about fishing. But the staff and its committee members did not fish.

Large, elaborate, and expensive training centers were built to teach fishermen how to fish. They taught fishing only. Year after year of tedious training, many students graduated and were given fishing licenses. They were sent out to do full-time fishing, some to distant waters teeming with fish. But like the fishermen back home, they never fished; these students engaged in all kinds of other occupations.

After one stirring meeting on the necessity of fishing, one young fellow left the meeting and actually went fishing. The next day he reported that he had caught two outstanding fish. He was honored for his excellent catch and was scheduled to visit all the big meetings possible to tell how he did it. So he stopped fishing in order to tell others about his fishing experience.

Now, it is true that many fishermen sacrificed and put up with all kinds of difficulty. Some lived near the water and bore the smell of dead fish every day; they received the ridicule of some who made fun of their fishermen's club and the fact that they claimed to be fishermen, but never fished. They wondered about those who felt that it was of little use to attend the weekly meetings to talk about fishing; after all, they were following the Master who said, "Follow Me and I will make you fishers of men." Imagine how hurt some of them felt when one day a person suggested that those who did not catch fish were not really fishermen, no matter what they claimed to be. Yet somehow . . . it really did sound correct. Is a person a fisherman if he never catches a fish? Is one following the Fisher of Men if he's not fishing?

Do you like to fish for the souls of men and women? I pray that God will turn us all into followers of Jesus who *love* to fish. Whenever we're at a restaurant, we bring out the hooks. Whenever we're at that board meeting, we get out the net. Let's just toss it out and see what the Lord does!

I'm telling you, the fishing is really, *really* good out there. It is! I've been there and I can tell you it is *so* refreshing. I could tell story after story, but I'll refrain. I'll just say that although the terrain may be difficult and the paths hard, all of us are on a mission from God. Each of us has a sphere of influence into which God tells us to "go."

So let's go . . . fishing!

Endnotes

Chapter 1

1. Ralph D. Winter and Bruce A. Koch, "Finishing the Task: The Unreached Peoples Challenge," *Mission Frontiers*, Pasadena, CA: June 2000, 22-33. William Carey Library:www.williamcareylibrary.gospelcom.net/ebooks/Finishing_The_Task.pdf.

2. Dr. James Kennedy, Evangelism Explosion, quoted in Paul Lee Tan, *Encyclopedia of 7700 Illustrations: Signs of the Times* (Rockville, MD: Assurance, 1979), 245.

Chapter 2

1. Michael Hodgin, *1002 Humorous Illustrations for Public Speaking* (Grand Rapids: Zondervan, 2004), 204.

2. Evelyn Underhill and Charles Lewis Slattery, *Concerning the Inner Life* (Whitefish, MT: Kessinger, 2003), 6-7.

Chapter 3

1. Pat Robertson, *Answers to 200 of Life's Most Probing Questions* (Nashville: Thomas Nelson, 1984), 96.

Chapter 4

1. “No Excuse Sunday,” *Sermon Humor*, http://hlw.www.50megs.com/Church/No_Excuse_Sunday/no_excuse_sunday.html.

2. William F. Buckley, Jr., “Empty Churches: Virtue in Denial,” *Religious Practice in National Review*, March 10, 1997.

3. Matt Redman, “Heart of Worship” lyrics, *Heart of Worship*, (EMI CMG Distribution, 1999).

4. New York Times, October 28, 1975, 68, quoted in Paul C. Vitz, *Psychology as Religion: The Cult of Self-Worship* (Grand Rapids: Wm. B. Eerdmans, 1994), 91.

5. “The Lord’s Supper Service,” *The Sermon Notebook*, 2003: www.sermonnotebook.org/new%20testament/1cor%20 11_17•34.htm.

Chapter 5

1. “Reuniting the Flock,” *U.S. News & World Report*, March 4, 1991, 50-51.

2. F.B. Meyer, *Alliance Weekly*, Sept. 26, 1925, 658.

3. Charles B. Williams, *Williams New Testament*, (Chicago: Moody, 1972).

Chapter 6

1. Dr. Walter T. Brown, *In the Beginning: Compelling Evidence for Creation and the Flood*, (Phoenix: Center for Scientific Creation, 2001), 3.

2. Ibid.

3. Henry F. Harlow, "The Nature of Love," *American Psychologist*, vol. 13, December 1958: 673-685.

Chapter 7

1. "Survey Shows How Christians Share Their Faith," *The Barna Update*, January 31, 2005. The Barna Group: www.barna.org/FlexPage.aspx?Page=BarnaUpdate&BarnaUpdateID=181. Used with permission.

2. Pastor Leon Johnson, "The House of God," www.bethesdabible.com/pdf/the%20house%20of%20god.pdf.

Chapter 8

1. Richard Lederer, "Questions & Answer: These Student Bloopers Are All Genuine, Authentic and Untouched," *National Review*, Dec. 31, 1995.

2. "Only Half of Protestant Pastors Have a Biblical Worldview," *The Barna Update*, January 12, 2004. The Barna Group: www.barna.org/FlexPage.aspx?Page=BarnaUpdate&BarnaUpdateID=156. Used with permission.

3. James Montgomery Boice, *Foundations of the Christian Faith: A Comprehensive & Readable Theology* (Downers Grove, IL: Intervarsity, 1986), 25-26.

4. Harvard Divinity School, *History and Mission Statement*, www.hds.harvard.edu/history.html.

5. Michael J. Vlach, "Americans and the Bible: Bible Ownership, Reading, Study and Knowledge in the United States," *Theological Studies*, www.theologicalstudies.citymax.com/page/page1572910.htm.

Chapter 9

1. Susan Gilbert, "Social Ties Reduce Risk of a Cold," *New York Times*, June 25, 1997.

2. John F. Havlik, *People-Centered Evangelism* (Nashville: Broadman, 1971).

3. Dr. Donald M. Joy, *Bonding: Relationships in the Image of God* (Nappanee, IN: Evangel Publishing House, 1997), 11-18.

Chapter 10

1. C. S. Lewis, *Mere Christianity* (New York: Harper Collins, 2001), 134.

2. Keith Miller & Bruce Larson, *The Edge of Adventure: An Experiment in Faith* (Waco, TX: Word Books, 1974), 156.

Chapter 11

1. Roger Martin, R.A. *Torrey: Apostle of Certainty* (Murfreesboro: Sword of the Lord, 2000), 166.

2. James P. Moore, *One Nation Under God* (New York: Doubleday, 2007).

Chapter 12

1. John Piper, *Let the Nations Be Glad! The Supremacy of God in Missions* (Grand Rapids: Baker Academic, 1993/2003), 17.

Chapter 13

1. A.W. Tozer, *Gems from Tozer* (Camp Hill, PA: Christian Publications, 1969), 13.

2. Ravi Zacharias & Norman Geisler, *Is Your Church Ready?* (Grand Rapids: Zondervan, 2003), 86.

3. Kenneth W. Osbeck, *101 Hymn Stories: The Inspiring True Stories Behind 101 Favorite Hymns* (Grand Rapids: Kregel, 1982), 14.

4. "Sing for Your Heart," *Heart Research UK*, www.heartresearch.org.uk/Singing is good for you.htm.

5. Andrew Coburn, "What Are We Doing on Sunday? One Church's Journey," *Interact Magazine*, Vol. 10, No. 2, 1999. Christian Growth Ministries: http://cgm.org.au/interact/1999v10n2/1999v10n2a2.html.

Chapter 14

1. Hollis Green, *Why Churches Die* (Dayton, TN: Global Educational Advance, 2007), 81.

2. JC Ryle, "Luke 8:16-21," *Grace Gems*, www.gracegems.org/Ryle/l08.htm.

3. Kenneth S. Wuest, *The New Testament: An Expanded Translation* (Grand Rapids: Eerdmans, 1961/1994).

4. John F. Piper, Jr. and John F. Piper, Robert Speer: *Prophet for the American Church* (Louisville: Geneva, 2000), 244.

5. "The Bournemouth," William Temple Association, www.williamtemple.org.uk/aboutwilliamtemple.html.